MARK SKAIFE

Affirmpress
books that leave an impression

Published by Affirm Press in 2020
28 Thistlethwaite Street, South Melbourne VIC 3205
www.affirmpress.com.au
10 9 8 7 6 5 4 3 2 1

Text and copyright © Mark Skaife, 2020
All rights reserved. No part of this publication may be reproduced without prior permission of the publisher.

Title: Mark Skaife / Mark Skaife, author
ISBN: 9781922400178 (hardback)

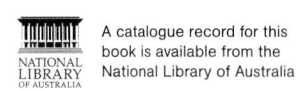

A catalogue record for this book is available from the National Library of Australia

Case and jacket design by Luke Causby, Blue Cork
Jacket image by Robert Cianflone/Getty Images
Case image courtesy of Aaron Noonan/an1images.com
Internal design and typesetting by Julian Mole, Post Prepress
Printed in China by C&C Offset Printing Co., Ltd.

Portrait of a racing legend featuring photographs from Mark's private collection, plus toasts and roasts from the racing people who know him best

MARK SKAIFE

THE COMPLETE ILLUSTRATED AUTOBIOGRAPHY OF ONE OF AUSTRALIA'S MOST SUCCESSFUL TOURING CAR DRIVERS EVER

Affirm press

CONTENTS

Introduction	1
Chapter 1 – It's in the blood	**3**
The Skaifes	5
Mark from Wyong	8
Team is family	9
That'll get your heart racing	13
Two kids hooning out behind the pits	16
Risky business	17
Pack your own bags	20
Chapter 2 – A taste for racing	**25**
On the road	28
A taste of success	32
Winning in reverse	38
MS – the Olympic-level talker	40
Chapter 3 – Gaining momentum (the Gibson years)	**43**
Learning lessons … and patience	47
When Dad and I left Nissan	54
Jim was no gentleman on the track	58
That fateful pairing	63
The guinea pig	66
Timing, the old way	69
The car named Godzilla	70
The biggest crash of my life	76
Chapter 4 – The turning point	**81**
Make or break	82
The mindset	86
Our first Bathurst win together	87
Picking up speed	90
The year of 115 days in a race car	96

Chapter 5 – A new era — 99

- *That* Bathurst — 102
- *Quelle* bloody *horreur* — 108
- International man of mystery — 112
- The Holden switch – and sweet revenge — 117
- The most satisfying title: 1994 — 120
- Random draw set up another win — 121
- Moments that make you question it all — 124
- No smoke, no fire — 127
- My very first motorsport chauffeur — 132
- Mark Skaife was different — 136

Chapter 6 – The fierce competitor (the HRT years) — 139

- Build the best team, then put a fence around it — 140
- Two Brocks — 147
- The friend and family man — 150
- Finding my feet with HRT — 155
- Lowndes and Skaife: chalk and cheese — 156
- He was always going to make it — 159
- The obsessive over-achiever — 160
- The three-peat — 165
- The most special Bathurst win — 177
- The perfect storm — 178
- It's all about commitment — 182
- Overtaking – a short story — 186
- An icon in motorsport's golden era — 188

Chapter 7 – The end of an era — 191

- Happy birthday Todd, let's win Bathurst — 194
- More than a mate: a brother — 197
- A gut-wrenching failure — 200
- There's a whole other book in these two years — 205
- Thirty years of getting 'Skaifed' — 210
- I wasn't doing a Brock, but it wasn't over — 218
- Three out of four ain't bad — 220

We went out and went *bang*	227
Skaifey – from enemies to friends!	230
My mate, Stupe	231

Chapter 8 – Life after racing   233

My new team	234
'You blokes must be kidding yourselves …'	238
The devil is in the detail	244
The gifted race caller	245
Get out of the chair and onto the track	246
My real family	251
Circuit design	258
Skaife: an epic dynasty of Australian motorsport	266

Mark Skaife chronology and key career statistics   267

1967 – 1990	270
1991 – 1995	271
1996 – 2002	272
2003 – 2009	273
2004 – 2017	274
Key career statistics	275
Australian touring car/V8 supercar championship overview	275
Complete Bathurst 1000 results	277
Acknowledgements	279
Image credits	280

INTRODUCTION

I was lucky in my driving career to drive with the three best teams of each era, starting with Gibson Motorsport, then Holden Racing Team and finally with Triple Eight. When I look back at what made them so good, I see they reflected the core values that my parents and grandparents taught me – good work ethic and good people were, and remain, critical components of success.

From a cultural perspective, each of the teams was a bit different in terms of how they approached the racing, but they all put in the time and effort, and the owners of each spent a lot of time trying to get the right staff and then retain them. In reality, it is no different to what Mum and Dad did with their business, Tyretown in Wyong. Today I also see that 'team' aspect in my TV work and pretty much everything I have been involved with post-racing. In particular, the track design engineering people at iEDM – specifically John Howe and his crew – have exactly that attitude and diligence.

In TV if you want to put together the best telecast, you need the best people; ones who are willing to sacrifice their own time to make it work.

I look back now and think of all those people that have helped me so much, and those who have been willing to go above and beyond to get either a result on the track, or a new sponsorship deal, or an improved component on the car done overnight, or whatever it is. Conquering the challenges that I faced through the course of my career really came down to what those people were willing to do to help me, and how hard they tried to achieve the best outcome.

A lot of the people who have contributed to this book are my closest confidants; they've been there for me through thick and thin. They're people for whom I have the highest admiration and respect. I value relationships, and I've been blessed by these relationships and what they have brought to me both professionally and personally.

I'm incredibly proud and honoured that so many of those people have been willing to recount some of our stories.

My grandfather Herb and me at a formal function. We always got on famously, but he also knew how to be honest with me when I wasn't working or racing at my best.

CHAPTER 1

IT'S IN THE BLOOD

I grew up on the Central Coast of New South Wales in a town called Wyong. We were a very sporty family. Initially for me it was Rugby League while my sister, Lisa, was into ballet and competition dressage horses. But racing was a natural extension of our family's connection to the motor industry. Dad started first and then encouraged me to get into karting, and that was it. This was *our* passion.

Top: Here's Dad and my grandfather outside Tyretown in Wyong. The lessons from my time with them in this place were nothing short of formative for me.

Bottom left: Tyretown living up to its good old name with one million tyre cases ready for retreading.

Bottom right: My grandfather having a beer at the spare parts counter on a Friday afternoon.

THE SKAIFES

I feel very privileged to have been part of a family that was committed to doing things well. My grandparents had a remarkable work ethic and were a big influence on me, as were my mum, Gay, and dad, Russell. My sister, Lisa, also benefited from their examples and has always been an incurable over-achiever, in and out of the world of motorsport. We were quite a unique family in some ways because our lives were centred on the family business, which my grandfather and grandmother built.

Pop grew up in Proserpine, which is about 300km north of Townsville, where we go racing today. After World War II, he and Nan moved to Newcastle where he worked for a rubber company, which was connected to a tyre business in Gosford. An opportunity came up to take over a service station in the rural town of Wyong, on the Central Coast of New South Wales, so he jumped in and did that and turned it into a lot more than just a service station. It was kind of like an automotive shop that did tyres, and then eventually tyres became the most important part of the business.

Eventually it turned into Tyretown. I got on really well with Pop, and I loved working with him even when I was young. He worked so hard in the early days of that business, which all his mates will tell you. It wasn't massively profitable to sell a set of tyres, so you had to sell a heap of them. When the time came to spend that profit, he was very diligent – I don't think he ever wasted a dollar. The post-war times in places like Wyong weren't easy, and Pop and Nan understood what they had to do to survive.

Their work ethic and understanding of the value of a dollar were my two most important takeaways from Pop and Nan; I knew if I wanted to get anywhere in life, I'd have to work hard for it. But that doesn't mean not enjoying what you do – as I said, I cherished those early years at the shop with Pop.

I think the other thing I took away from that time was the sense of community you get in rural Australia. Looking back on it, there is no doubt that it's stronger there than in the city, and it did make things easier for my grandparents. The locals always supported their community and the sense of mateship was amazing.

The Aussie battler is entrenched in the national psyche, and for me the battler is someone like Pop, selling tyres and automotive services in a town like Wyong.

I still feel a little bit of the pull to my home town. I am regularly in contact with the guys I grew up with, and I just love heading back that way when the Supercars race in Newcastle. I can always find someone on the Central Coast to have a beer with. Wyong sits halfway between Newcastle and what was once Amaroo Park, so even though we weren't in Sydney, when we started to get into motorsport it was easy to head down and watch some racing on what was a great little track.

For me, that sense of community transferred to my racing. I still talk to the guys I played footy with, I still talk to the guys in the teams I went racing with and today my little extended family is the TV crew. It is the rapport we have all built that allows it to work so easily.

I think in the end all businesses are people businesses. Motorsport is profoundly that: it's about people's effort, it's about their willingness to go above and beyond, and if you've got that camaraderie and rapport it all has a chance to work. I am lucky today to work with guys like Neil Crompton and Mark Larkham who work bloody hard to get the best show possible. So much thought and dedication goes into telling a story each weekend and taking the viewer on a journey. That narrative doesn't just happen, and if you can get it all together and make a complex game sound as simple as possible, you have done a really good job. They do that.

I am lucky too. As I said, I learned the value of hard work, but I have also had many people on the journey with me who were just as willing to work hard – to go that extra mile because it would help the cause. Many of them were as competitive as I am. As I have said many times, I am a very below average loser and most of the people I've built that connection with were the same. That shared mentality bonded us; it made our losses all the more miserable but, knowing the heart that the team put into their work, the wins couldn't have been sweeter.

Top Left: A young Nan and Pop.

Middle and bottom left: Little bloke pictures at eighteen months old at my grandparents' house on the river front in Wyong. The family business was never far away from our family life – as you can tell by those tyres in the background.

Top right: A little older here, mucking around with cars at Mum and Dad's first house.

Bottom right: Sharing time with my younger sister, Lisa.

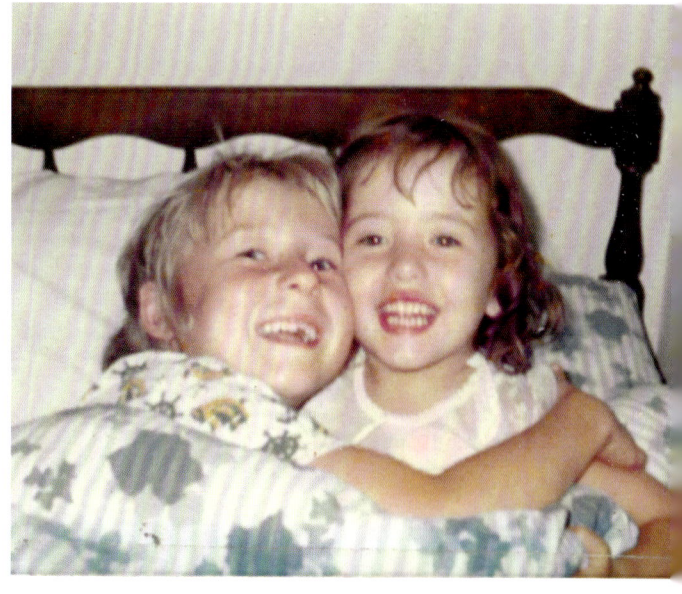

IT'S IN THE BLOOD

MARK FROM WYONG
Words by Steve Crawley, Head of Television, Fox Sports

Mark Skaife and I text or email each other a fair bit, and he always signs off 'Mark from Wyong'.

That's because we're both from the Central Coast of New South Wales, me from Gosford and he, well, you already know – he's from Wyong! Wyong folk are tough bastards, especially the ones who play for the Kangaroos, which Mark did when he was a kid, scoring more than the odd try out at Morry Breen Field where Gosford townies were often mugged.

Skaifey's parents ran the tyre joint in the main street, opposite where you turn off to the racecourse, and everyone knew his old man Russell because he raced touring cars and his picture was always in the sporting pages of *The Advocate*.

What everyone didn't know was the work ethic of one Gay Skaife, Mark's mum, who sat in the middle office, forever arriving first, leaving last and doing just about everything in between. That's exactly where Mark got it from. ◎

Mum and Dad's Brock Commodore parked in front of the tyre business in Wyong. A sign of things to come?

TEAM IS FAMILY

To build a team, you bring people in – you don't cast them aside. You need to keep it on task and not be personal. You can say that *it's* just not good enough, not that *you're* not good enough. You don't actually say that someone is a goose because they made a mistake, but you look at what went wrong and how to prevent it from happening again.

There's a real delineation in how you treat people based on that team rapport and dynamic. Motor racing's a weird game if you think about it, with the team having to operate like a family: we were always on the same aeroplane, in the same hotel, the same rental car and we even ate together … it was pretty tight.

That harks right back to my earliest memories in the tyre business. We had some employees who were with us for 20 years or more who were just welded on and really loyal. We knew their wives and their families. Dad would have barbecues at home and staff would come, and I reckon my attitude to kinship in motorsport came from that.

We never went on holidays when I was a kid because we always made more money over Christmas than any other time. I mean, this was a business that was turning over $400,000 a month way back in the late 1980s. It was a bloody good business.

In those times around Christmas, because we were stuck between Sydney and Newcastle and the Central Coast was full of holidaymakers, we were flat out. If we'd wanted to have 30 or 40 people working for us fixing tyres and cars at that time we could have kept them all busy, but we only had 15 or 20 in that client-facing part of the business. We ended up with about 50 or 60 staff all up and a couple of different sites with different retail shops, but the original one in Wyong was at the heart of it all.

Because we were so busy in those times, it really affected whatever we did outside work. Playing footy, or karting or whatever, had to be done without harming the business. I still remember when I was only 17 or 18 driving all the way back with the old man from a Laser race in Winton, in the middle of Victoria, on a Sunday night so we could open the door at eight o'clock on a Monday morning.

That work ethic and, as hard as it was, accepting Dad's rules of engagement, have carried me through life.

So Pop built the business and Dad took over in about 1973, and he changed it from a specialised tyre shop, where we basically did tyres and batteries, into a more general auto business. Dad's a really bright guy and he made it work and grow on the back of the things he'd learned from Pop. He made a spare parts business first, which he combined with a mechanical repair business that was just outstanding. We were the first ones up in Wyong with a good wheel alignment machine and were the specialists in suspension and brake machining. We were also the first ones in town with proper hoists and pipe benders to make exhausts. Additionally we were one of the first to do hydraulic hoses with proper crimping tools. It was just a ripping business.

My grandfather had no interest in racing at all – zero. In fact when Dad started racing, Pop thought it was a waste of money. There was plenty of evidence that my grandfather was really tough, and when Dad decided that he was going to do some car racing, Pop thought this hobby thing was distracting him from the business, and they clashed over that. But Dad always did his own thing, and he made good money because he worked hard and had the intelligence to carry off his ideas. His first road car was a Holden EH S4, which was like buying an HSV car – that was a seriously good car for the time, and many say it was the car that started the Supercar era in Australia. It showed how strong the business was.

We didn't live in the flashest house, but thanks to my parents' hard work we had really nice things. We even ended up having a swimming pool out the back and lots of kids would come around and hang out during the warmer weather. Mum was fastidious, and she spent every weekend making sure that all our cars were as tidy as the house.

The business was good enough to sustain me in karting and car racing, and it bought Lisa an array of dressage horses and everything she needed to compete at the highest levels. We never did anything by halves. We worked hard, but we played hard too, which was great. I learned a lot from that approach.

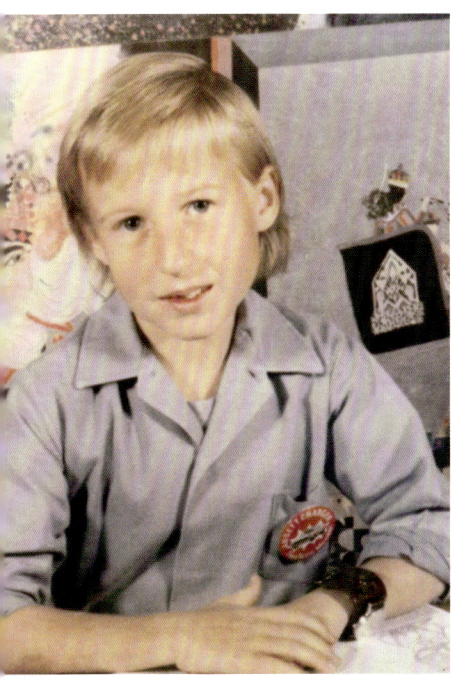

The common theme with these shots is average haircuts.

Top left: Do you reckon I could get my strides any higher? In my uniform for Wyong Primary School.

Top right: My first school class photo in 1972. I'm in the second row from the front, second boy from the left.

Bottom right: Here's Lisa, aged six, and me, aged eight, standing in front of Dad's L34 Torana.

Bottom left: A school photo from Wyong Primary School.

IT'S IN THE BLOOD   11

Top left: In typical fashion, the old man bought a bike that was way too big for me – but he always wanted to buy the coolest thing of the day.

Top right: My eighth birthday party with Lisa by my side, critiquing my candle-blowing technique.

Bottom left and right: The lads playing footy in our front yard.

THAT'LL GET YOUR HEART RACING

Some of my earliest memories are of me on Dad's shoulders at the car racing tracks in Sydney, Amaroo Park and Oran Park. I know I was at Warwick Farm too, but I only really have limited memory of that. I remember being on his shoulders at the dogleg at Oran Park, which was one of the great corners in Australian motorsport. The difference between the good blokes and bad blokes across there was just incredible.

I remember sitting in the grandstand at the final corner at Oran Park, at what was called Energol and then turned into BP, and being under Amaroo Park's Ron Hodgson tower at the final corner – the one with the media centre above it – watching all the best drivers go through. I just loved it, and not only because Dad was racing some of the time. I started to appreciate the drivers' skills; I watched the very best drivers and started to understand who was good, who wasn't and why. It was the way they turned the wheel, the way they applied the correction and their throttle control and all the beautiful things about their technique.

When I wasn't with Dad I was with Glenn Seton, who was just two years older than me, and we loved mucking about behind the pits and watching the action unfold. I reckon this must be how a junior footballer learns from the masters of the game. You watch a Joey Johns, a Bob Fulton or a Wally Lewis and you try to do the same things they do – and your technique and your style evolve as you accumulate more information.

Amaroo Park was a great track to watch car racing because there was plenty of elevation, and if you were standing in the right spot you could really see the drivers' hands at work. You could watch them from Dead Stop Corner and down into that last Ron Hodgson Corner, where you could see the car slide out to the Armco corner and look for the drivers who used every little bit of road. They'd be the ones dragging the mirror on the fences because the car was sliding out there – not because they were steering towards it.

If you were standing at the final corner, you were basically looking front-on so you could see how the car reacted when the driver applied steering to turn it in, and then you'd see it slide towards the kerb right in front of you and disappear against the Armco fence to go up the hill.

In a pretty short stretch of track you could see so much, but you could also hear them coming out of Dead Stop – the amount of wheelspin or the slide – and you heard them light up the throttle and apply their correction, or the steering reaction, through that corner. I just loved it. And the difference between what Pete Geoghegan and Colin Bond did, or Allan Moffat and Peter Brock, was great for me to dig into. It suited my analytical brain.

I remember saying to Dad once, 'Imagine if you could put all those attributes, the best of each of them, into one place. You'd have an amazing driver.' I always used to say that Allan Grice was the best braker and Colin Bond had the best overall car control. I loved the way Peter Brock turned the car at the corner, and Jimmy Richards seemed to have it all. In a weird way, when I started I was trying to embody that 'perfect' driver; I was using my own learnings to adapt and hoping I had the skill to do it.

I often think about how special it was to have watched superstars like Moffat, Richards, Brock, Grice, Bond and Bob Morris as a young bloke, and then actually got a chance to race against them. I'm really lucky that the timing of my career made this possible before the next era of drivers took over.

Everyone in motorsport talks about the average driver's age coming down and the life expectancy of their professional career not being as long as it used to be. But back then, people would be saying Colin Bond, Dick Johnson, Allan Moffat and Peter Brock – all those superstars – should retire. But in my opinion they only needed to start thinking about that when the young blokes started to beat them – and when I was starting out that wasn't happening. They were more than holding their own. I never once thought those guys should stop because they were getting old. They were still fierce competitors.

Dad really encouraged me; he loved my infatuation with the sport and he knew how committed I was. I learned so much from him about cars and how to control them. One of my other earliest memories of the old man was of him letting me stand between the seats of the car while he was driving out in the country – unheard of today, but back then it was okay and possible too. If he ever had to brake hard, he just put his hand out to stop me from flying forward.

We did a lot of driving in those days because we serviced all of the farms outside Wyong. There are some beautiful places out there, from the Yarramalong and Dooralong Valleys up into the Hunter Valley, and we looked after all the truck and tractor tyres on those farms. We'd be blazing away out there on the country roads with Dad sliding around in the dirt and me watching it all: his feet, his hands, the lot.

One place I liked to watch Dad driving was at a property Nan and Pop developed on the Wyong River, a subdivision next to a beautiful old guesthouse called Strathaven. There was a dirt road there with a big and fast right-hander coming onto the property, and Dad was just into it every time we went there. There were other places where he liked to put on a bit of a show – he was great at sliding the car on the dirt; he had great car control.

I learned so much about that stuff from Dad and from watching how he did it. He always told me when it came to opposite lock you should never apply too much, and that the art of correcting it was what everyone got wrong. 'The art,' he rightly said, 'is getting the lock off fast enough.' That's what helps you avoid the big tank slappers you see the goons have when they get it wrong.

Close family friends Peter and Rod Tillett with Dad and me. We used to ride motorcycles out in the valley behind Wyong.

TWO KIDS HOONING OUT BEHIND THE PITS
Words by Glenn Seton, former racing driver and childhood friend

Mark was pretty fiery and very ambitious, even as far back as when I first met him. My dad started racing Ford Capris in 1975, and when he upgraded his car for 1976, he sold the old one to Russell Skaife and that is when I first met Mark. He was nine and I was eleven.

Russell raced that Capri for a couple of years, and we became very close family friends and Mark became a good mate of mine. We spent a hell of a lot of time together at the racetracks while our fathers were racing. We'd spend most of the time at the back in the pit areas, hanging out with each other, and then sitting up on the hill at Amaroo Park watching our dads race.

When they weren't watching, we'd grab one of their road cars and go for a hoon out the back of the pit areas at Amaroo and Oran Park. We got to know each other pretty well during that phase.

I started karts at the age of 14, and because Mark is two years younger he was pretty much starting when I was finishing. Once I semi-finished in karts, we sort of transferred over all my gear, even my racing leathers, which he initially used. We spent a lot of time at each other's places during that transition.

Mark was always very determined and very loud, like his dad, which was great because it meant there was never a dull moment with the Skaife family.

I was probably a calming influence for him and helped keep him out of trouble. I'm not loud; I'm very introverted and he is just the opposite, and that worked well for us as kids and through our racing as well. Under it all was respect for each other. He accepted I was quiet and I accepted he was loud and that kept our relationship together for so many years.

RISKY BUSINESS

When I look back at a place like Amaroo Park, I never remember thinking about what it took to race there and the risk involved in driving something as fast as a Formula Holden. It was a wild little track. It looked so simple on paper but in reality was amazingly complex, and any miscalculation had consequences.

The run up Bitupave Hill and down through the Dunlop Loop was as good as anything we have in Australian motorsport, and it felt like you were constantly turning with little room for error. Not to mention the run from Dead Stop Corner – a weird little off-camber piece that sucked you out the wall with not a millimetre between the track and concrete fence, which lined the track all the way to the pit entry and then Armco out past the pit exit.

Hindsight's a ridiculous thing, isn't it? Looking back now, I think, *What the hell was I doing?* But back then I didn't think, I just did it. In the Formula Holden we were as quick as anything that had ever raced there – up to eight to ten seconds a lap quicker than a touring car with lap times into the low forties for a nearly two-kilometre lap – but you never thought about anything other than how to go faster while you were at the wheel.

I had watched a lot of racing there, as had Dad. In the Formula Holden you had to go flat all the way to the top of the hill before dropping down the Dunlop Loop, then it was flat again all the way through Suttons and down to Honda.

Dad said to me one day, after watching me driving the Formula Holden at practice, that I had to be really careful with the left-hand rear wheel against the guardrail as I turned into the kink next to the control tower. He thought it was getting so close that I was going to clip the Armco, and that was not going to be nice. I had no idea – eyes forward as they say.

If I had hit it, it would have fired me straight into the fence and I'd be dead. No middle ground: dead. By that stage in my career, Dad didn't give me too much advice on driving, so when he delivered that message to me I knew it must have been pretty serious and that he was worried, so I paid attention. Dad was pretty much like me: he knew the risks and knew what he thought I was capable of, and this was the only time he legitimately felt I needed a safety warning.

Above: Me aged six, with Dad's XU-1 in 1973 and his one-tonne ute in the background at Oran Park.

Left: At Dad's office in Tyretown, the family business. You can see pictures of my early go-karting and of Dad's Capri in the background.

I remember another time at Amaroo when he got Ivan Stibbard from the ARDC to give me dispensation to start at the back of the grid of a sports sedan race in the rain even though I hadn't done any laps in practice. If that was my son, no way. But he was okay. Wouldn't happen today anyway; it was a dangerous joint at the best of times, but in the rain the water ran down the hill like a river and it was wild. But on that day, Dad sealed up the car – anywhere water might get in, he taped it over – and he sent me out with the best tyres we could get at the time.

I started seventeenth and finished sixth with the fourth-fastest lap. I absolutely loved it, and I had such a big smile on my face that he was rapt too. It showed the relationship we had at the time, and still do. If he thought I could handle something he was the first to back me, but if he thought I was overstepping he wouldn't hold back. He was pretty honest with me all the time, and that was good, if sometimes a little brutal. He wanted to know I'd put my best foot forward each time I did something, whether it was at work, on the rugby league field or car racing.

I reckon that's where there's a massive disparity between fathers who get it and fathers who don't. The stereotypical father in car racing thinks their son is the next Ayrton Senna, yet they are so far off in terms of understanding the reality of either the talent or the effort required to get there. My old man just wasn't in that camp. In the end though I think I was ultimately harder on myself than he, or anyone else for that matter, ever was.

PACK YOUR OWN BAGS

My penchant for preparation and leaving nothing to chance came mostly from Mum, with a little bit of Dad. If you went to her place right now, you'd see this amazing level of detail in everything she has and everything she does. When it came to racing karts Dad and I never really employed anyone to help us – except for when it came to the engines, which Ken Mitchell in Sydney and then Don McLean helped with – so it was all down to me to get ready for racing.

After school I would come home and work on the kart, either at the workshop or in the partly converted carport at home. On a Thursday, if we were racing that weekend, I had to be packed and ready to go. I was doing my own inventory back then; if I wanted to race I had to make sure I had everything I needed, so I made a system to make sure I remembered everything, and I'd tick it all off as I packed my bags and loaded the trailer. I say the same thing to my kids today: if you want to play sport then you have to make sure you have everything packed, or you won't play.

I was 14 when that was all happening, and it was a great time. There was a round of the World Championships at Cockburn in Western Australia. That was an unbelievable racetrack, and I reckon kids came from everywhere for it. An Italian team called IAME was offering the top-ranked local kid the use of one of their Parilla engines for the weekend. The engine prefix was a TT27 SSHK and I wanted it so badly.

All the stuff was air-freighted over there, which made Don a bit nervous. I reckon he asked a dozen times on the flight over if I had everything. I did, and I got the engine too. It was a great engine and I think I finished third with it, behind a couple of international drivers, but I didn't get to keep it.

With karting, it wasn't like the lights flashed and sparks were flying for me. I was good, but not that good. Really, I think the first time I properly drove one was at Newcastle with a roughly 20-second lap. Two brothers, Shane and Steven Boyd, were the young guns we were aiming to beat. I was with Glenn Seton and he went out and did a 19.2, which was a second quicker, and that was huge. The best I could do was a 20.2, which was a fair way off, but I was two years younger and less experienced than Glenn – or so I kept telling myself.

Left: Aged 13 at the Hawkesbury River in Windsor. Clearly a skinny little runt with a body more suited to car racing than footy.

Below: Scrawny as I was, I loved playing footy. Here's Wyong Rugby League Club Under 15s, and that's me in the front giving cheek.

IT'S IN THE BLOOD 21

Pop may not have agreed with Dad and me getting into racing, but that didn't stop him being a big supporter over the years.

Top left: With Dad and Pop at Christmas 1986 at the end of my first year in Melbourne.

Top right: Pop and Nan visiting me at my first house, in Mt Eliza. I'd flown them down to see a show on Collins St.

Middle left: Pop and me in 1993, at my wedding to my first wife, Belinda (my son Mitch's Mum).

Below: Some of my best mates, (left to right) Gavin Wand, Anthony Tratt and Rod Smith, were also there for me through many years to come. Here they are as groomsmen at my first wedding.

When I eventually did a race at Newcastle I spun out of three of the five races – you know, typical shit on cold tyres with no experience. But the next week was at Oran Park and it rained and I won. I went from a disastrous Newcastle in the dry to a win in the rain at Sydney and I remember thinking: *I'm better at this than I am at playing footy*. That was the first time I'd genuinely felt that way, and I started to move away from footy and into the karts.

Dad was great with it: his level of preparation and desire to do it were right off the charts. He plucked the master cylinder off the kart and had it stainless-steel-sleeved to make the piston size smaller and the pedal travel longer to get more brake feel. We were doing shit that no-one else was doing – and that sort of stuff was fundamental to my learning because it actually gave me the chance to feel the changes. We'd make a change and send me out, and if I came back in and said I couldn't feel it he had no problem. But if he thought I was trying to bullshit him just to make him feel good about it, then we'd have an issue. Fundamentally I just had to straight up tell the truth.

I've always had a theory that some people have greater natural aptitude to an activity than others. You see that innate ability in all forms of sport and other disciplines around you. The people who succeed are the ones who take that ability and commit all the effort required to go to the next level. If you have enough of both you can be a superstar, but you've got to be honest with yourself and those you are working with.

Looking very young here as I await my driving stint in Peter Williamson's Toyota Supra in the 1986 Castrol 500 at Sandown, Melbourne.

CHAPTER 2

A TASTE FOR RACING

Karting was one thing, but when I moved into cars I felt like that was more me. My competitive nature meant I wasn't going to be half-arsed about it either, and from the very start Dad was keen to do it right too. He worked out what sort of car we needed, then found one and virtually had it rebuilt from scratch. Until I started driving professionally, this was how we did it – we sourced from and used the best people for each job, and it worked.

My first racing car was this Torana XU-1, here at Amaroo Park. It was great for learning some race craft and did the job we bought it for.

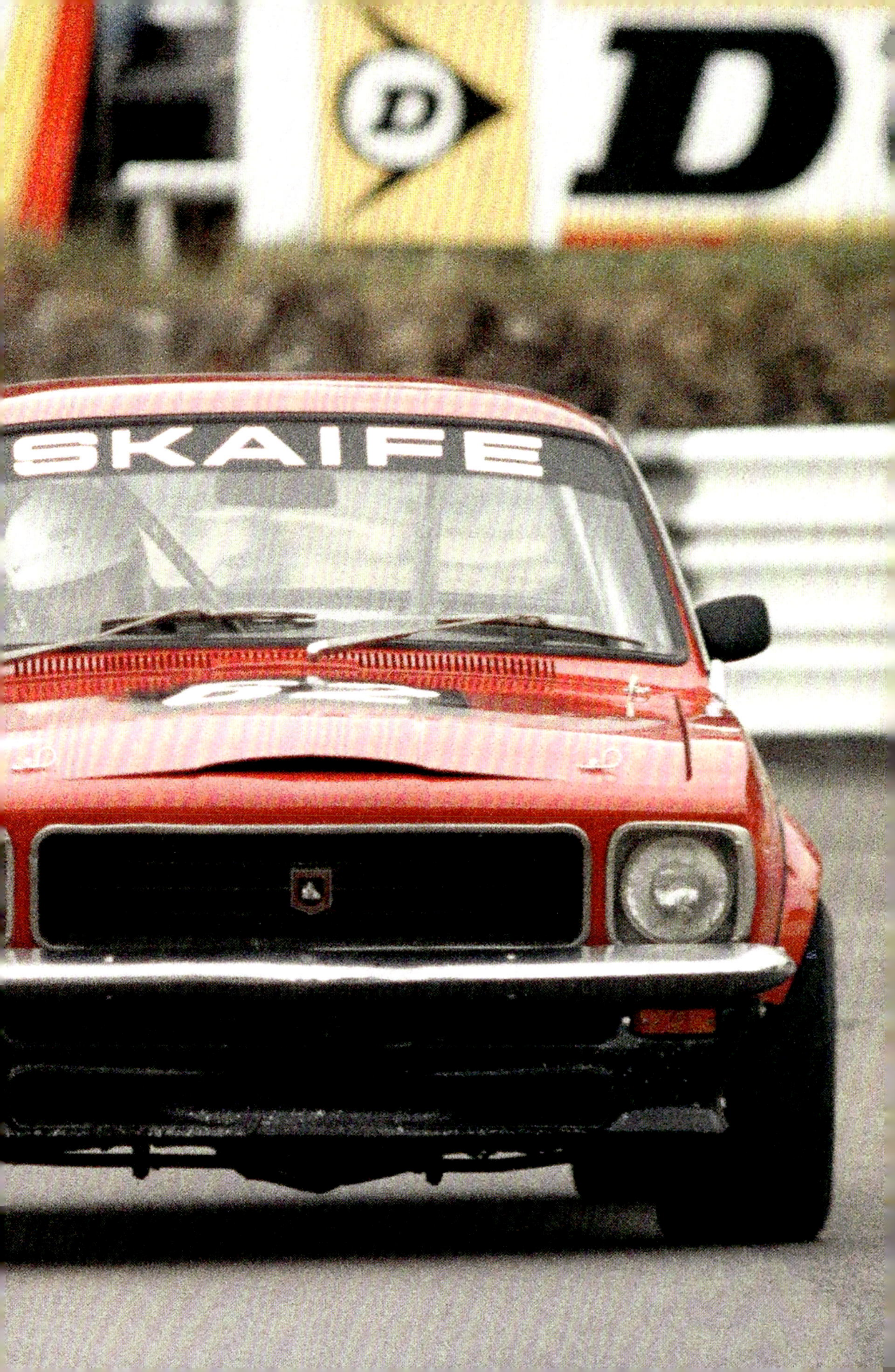
SKAIFE

ON THE ROAD

Moving from karts to cars was a big thing. For a start it was more expensive and it involved different tracks. We were flat out at the time with the family business, and we needed to start hiring other people to help with the car racing. Dad had obviously been around a bit and he knew a lot of people, but he had a few blues with Pop over the money he was spending, not to mention what we lost by not being at the shop.

I was always a year or two behind Glenn Seton, and he'd made the step into cars and was doing quite well by the time I was making the move. I did my licence test in his Ford Capri and almost spun at Suttons at Amaroo Park when I tried to do something that would have been normal in a kart, but was not acceptable in a car. I had a bit to learn, that was for sure.

Aside from the bills getting bigger and the machines needing different technique, you didn't go about it the same way you'd go about karting and we had to learn on the run. Even to this day I don't think we do a good job of transitioning young drivers from karts to cars. I think we fundamentally price some people out of it at the junior levels, which fortunately didn't happen to me, and that no doubt shrinks the talent pool we see on the track.

We wanted a six-cylinder sports sedan for my first race car and there were lots of good cars in the Sydney club racing scene at the time. Dad looked around for a while and we ended up buying a Torana XU-1 for $4000 from Jim Winterbottom, Mark Winterbottom's father. That became a real project for us. When we got the car it hadn't been raced for a while, so we basically dismantled it and then started to rebuild it step-by-step. Barry Seton did the engine, which had 259 horsepower, and we bought some ex-Bob Morris XU-1 stuff and did a fair bit of work on it.

It was a bloody good car when we'd finished; I mean in a big field of cars at Oran Park, I qualified on the front row against all the V8s. Oran Park and Amaroo Park were not power tracks, but they were good places to learn. Most of my racing was done at those two tracks, but I did have a run at Lakeside once because Barry Seton thought we should. We drove the 1000 kilometres or so to get there, and within half an hour we had blown the engine and had to come home. A cruel lesson.

I never really crashed that car, but I did have a massive spin in the rain coming up the ramp of the dogleg at Oran Park when I was dicing for the lead with Mal Rose – that was the closest I came to seriously damaging it. It was raining so hard that the water had puddled up against the inside kerb but you couldn't see it from the car. I fired up the ramp (as I called it) at the start of the dogleg and the front right-hand wheel caught the puddle, spinning me sideways and I went off at the top of the hill and into the grass. Somehow I didn't hit the fence; I was basically kissed because it was totally out of control. That was my first big spin, and thankfully Dad was totally fine about it, but it was pretty frightening at the time.

I was learning heaps. Dad was great with the feedback, but I hadn't yet developed my own thing. I had in my head that I wanted to be the perfect race driver, but at this stage I really just had to learn about cars. No-one was in the car with me and there was no data to follow – I had to develop all of that feel myself without going so far that I damaged the car.

I did the XU-1 for about a year, then the Laser Series was announced and we headed down that path.

Dad in his XU-1 on the Dunlop Loop at Amaroo Park in 1974.

A TASTE FOR RACING

Above: In the paddock at the 1985 Laser Series, Oran Park.

Left: In the first year of the Ford Laser Series (1985) leading two of the best series production drivers of the day: Mark Gibbs and Peter Dane. When the Laser Series started we sold the XU-1 and immediately jumped into the new one make series. It was to be one of the best motor racing decisions I ever made. I won the Victorian Series and was twice runner-up in NSW, but it was here that Fred Gibson came to watch me race.

Following Mark Gibbs into Dead Stop Corner, Amaroo Park. The racing in the Laser Series was great despite them not being the best race car. Pretty sure I didn't touch Mark here ... but who knows?

A TASTE FOR RACING 31

A TASTE OF SUCCESS

The Laser Series came along in 1985 when I was 18, and it was a great opportunity for a young bloke. It was a bit like the Toyota 86 Series of today, only cheaper. Ford heavily discounted the cars, and Goodyear and Motorcraft were putting in heaps. There were some really good drivers in that Laser Series – Mark Gibbs, Peter Dane, Steve Williams, David Brabham, Ken Douglas and Jim Zerefos were all excellent production car drivers. We all started out as pretty good mates and many of us actually worked alongside each other, preparing the cars together in Barry Jones's workshop in Sydney.

A lot of those guys were very experienced at driving those sorts of cars. Underpowered front-wheel-drive cars on standard road tyres are quite hard to drive, because you have to flow them and keep the momentum up to get good lap times. Being front-wheel-drive means they have a quirky nature too.

In the second year I was desperate to do the Victorian series as well as the Sydney one, and I remember sitting in Dad's office calling every Victorian Ford dealer to source the money to come down to Melbourne. Without that money we simply couldn't afford to do it.

In the end, a guy called Ron Kaplan from Stillwell Ford was the only one to show any interest. The only deal he said he could do was to match whatever I could win on the track. I had to run signage on the front mudguards, and if I didn't win any prize money I wouldn't get a cent from him.

The Sydney series had fantastic prize money at $3000 for a win, but the Victorian Motorcraft series was only $1000. We won every round in Melbourne and I kept sending invoices to Ron, and he'd laugh because he'd thought the deal would result in no more than his sign on the car of a young bloke from the Central Coast – and that it wouldn't cost him anything. At least he could laugh about it, even though it turned out to be quite expensive for him.

A lot of the Victorian rounds were also at big race meetings, so we got to race in front of the people we needed to race in front of. We played to our strengths and put a lot of effort into buffing the tyres and wheel alignments, as well as looking at the engines with Barry Jones. Bob Riley helped us with the other stuff like roll cages and other preparation.

Above: Tackling the infield section of the Sandown circuit in my Ford Laser in April 1986.

Right: Going into the Loop at Amaroo Park with Peter Dane in tow.

That series had a national TV broadcast and really good prize money; it ticked all the boxes we needed to tick at the time. It was way cheaper than Formula Ford and the racing was better too. I was also starting to learn the value of people in the paddock. I remember coming from last and winning at Sandown in the wet – that's $1000, thanks, Ron – and I'm sure important people were watching. Mum was there a lot and so we always had the best-presented and prepared car, which I'm sure people noticed too.

We were doing some fun commercial things with the business, which was allowing me to fund the racing. For instance, I'd bundle up and sell all the second-hand tyres that had come off cars if they were still any good – like with 50% of the tread or more intact. We did the hydraulics on a Bobcat one weekend. It was a three-grand job and my labour component went into the race car.

Meanwhile my schooling had fallen well away. I did my HSC but I was never there in class, and not doing that final year properly is one of my few regrets.

I came second in the New South Wales series in 1985 and then set out to win in 1986. I was in good shape and racing Peter Dane for the series lead at Oran Park in the second last round. I passed him at the final corner for the lead of the race and as we exited towards the wall, he punted me and I got cleaned up by others and wrote the car off. I would have been leading the series going into the final round, so I was just feral and I didn't talk to him for 25 years or more.

Anyway, we had to get a car ready for the next round, so Dad called Doug Jacobi, who was a Director at Ford and Head of Motorcraft, and got a body shell from him. I basically worked day and night for a week pulling everything that could be rescued out of the crashed car and fitting it to the new one. Then we had to buy whatever bits and pieces we needed to get it finished. We ended up rolling out a car that was half a chance and won. I actually thought in the end that it was a better car than the old one. Pity it was the end of the series.

With the points I lost at Oran Park, everything had to go my way to win the title. Essentially Dane had to have a shocker, so all I wanted was to win and see what happened from there. I had a great race. Steve Williams and I were side-by-side for almost a full lap, but I was on the wrong side – being the outside – the whole time. At one stage I came off the bottom of the Loop, still on the outside and heading into the fast right hander at Mazda House when I got a little bump that forced me into the dirt. When I rejoined it was just before the left hander at Honda, where I repaid the favour and knocked Steve into the dirt on the right and I took the lead and then the win.

Dad was happy with that move too – and seriously, it is still one of my best.

> **Here's an extract from Auto Action's *Race Report* that chronicles that moment:**
> *Skaife, unaccustomed to being led and wanting to grab all the series points he could, pulled alongside Williams and the war was on.*
>
> *For almost one lap the duo remained side-by-side and it was obvious that something had to give. It did! As they approached Honda Corner, Williams headed for the dirt and found himself in sixth place when he returned to the track.*
>
> *All was not peaches and cream for Skaife either as he also found himself on the grass, this time at the exit from Honda. Fortunately for him, the rest of the field was far enough back to allow him to re-join the race still in the lead.*

TOYOTA GENUINE
PARTS
77
Castrol 500
P. WILLIAMSON
M. SKAIFE
LIVERPOOL SMASH REPAIRS
Castrol

Here I am at the wheel of the Peter Williamson Toyota Supra in the 1986 Castrol 500 endurance race at Sandown. We finished 10th overall in the race, which my future Nissan teammates George Fury and Glenn Seton won.

WINNING IN REVERSE

Fred Gibson coming to watch me race was really because of Barry (Bo) Seton more than anything else. We were very close with the Setons, and Dad and Bo were good mates. In 1985 Bo's son Glenn had moved to Melbourne to join Gibson Motorsport, and he'd drive a Nissan for the team in 1986. Once he had those first couple of drives in the Bluebird he was basically entrenched in the new factory Nissan team that Fred had taken over.

Bo was always complimentary about how I was going and would say, 'You should have a look at this kid. He's doing a good job'. So Fred came to watch me on the day they did a mad reverse-direction race at Oran Park. Not a reverse grid – a reverse direction. And let me tell you, *that* was interesting. I got a knock and dropped to the back, but then fought my way through to win. I guess Fred was impressed because he offered me a job soon after.

The job was basically in the workshop with no promise of a drive, but I didn't hesitate because I knew that it was a good place to be. I could see how Glenn was going there, progressing his driving career, and I wanted that chance. If the opportunity to drive came up, I'd have a serious crack.

So, in September 1986 after a Laser race at Winton, which I won, I headed south to move in with the Setons while Dad and my girlfriend at the time headed north back to Wyong. I was 19. It was pretty emotional for all of us. It wasn't just the family separation; it was also the end of me having anything to do with the family business that my grandfather had started. Dad was a big supporter of the move to Melbourne because he knew what it could potentially mean.

I paid $50 a week in board to the Setons and I was getting paid $200 from Fred, so it was a pretty lean time. But the Setons were great – they were workaholics. Bo would often be in the engine room at Gibsons into the middle of the night, so Glenn and I were just doing stuff around the workshop. I had to learn to slow down, though. When I arrived, I started out rushing everywhere like I had been doing at home, where time was money and it was all rip, tear and bust. But here it was different.

Trevor Jones was one of the lead technicians and had worked for Fred for many years, and to this day is one of the smartest automotive people I've ever been around. His nickname was Bones and he used to yell at me to stop running. If I needed something I'd run – it was what I'd always done. But I needed to readjust. We used to clean the workshop back at Wyong each weekend – hose it out, effectively – but this set-up was different in that regard too. Everything in this place was pristine and the level of engineering was off the charts. We were the first ones to basically do all our stuff in-house, which was going to be really important in a few years' time.

But I knew where I stood. On the one-to-ten scale of automotive knowledge, I was a one and there were blokes in there that were nines and tens. Guys like Bones, Andrew Bartley, Ross Holder and obviously Barry Seton in the engine room were among the very best automotive minds anywhere. Fred was very strategic; he was very good at identifying where the car was deficient and applying fixes, and he made sure he had people around who were very clever in their specialisation.

There was a lot of high-level expertise and I really liked it. I fitted in, once I slowed down, and I was learning from the best. Early on, Fred invited me to dinner and I went to a little Italian restaurant with him, his wife Chrissie and their two girls, Shona and Tania. They made it easy to settle in. Chrissie was fantastic; she was like another mum to me.

I wanted to be on the track, not in the workshop developing cars for the special vehicles' division – though it made us a lot of money. There was a Nissan dealer named John Giddings, and he had us build a Gazelle for him to run in some races late in 1986, and I used that car to win the 1987 Australian 2.0 Litre Touring Car Championship. We won three out of the four rounds, so that was pretty satisfying, but I hungered for more.

For me, there was a very big difference between testing and racing, and I wanted to be racing, but the main squad had drivers like Glenn Seton, George Fury and even John Bowe, so I knew I'd have to wait. I was never very patient.

MS – THE OLYMPIC-LEVEL TALKER
Words by Fred Gibson, Australian racing driver and race team owner

The first thing I have to say about Mark is that he really hasn't changed much. I was watching him on TV just the other day and I said to my wife, Chris, 'Listen to Skaifey, waffling on here about bullshit …' He's articulate and analytical, but he bangs on a bit, and that's the way he's always been!

My relationship with Mark started when Chris and I moved to Melbourne to take over the Nissan team. I asked Barry Seton to come down south with us to prepare the engines, and he insisted that in order to make that happen I would have to find a role for his son Glenn, and I did.

In fact Bo and Glenn were a big part of the huge rebuilding job we had to do, because it really was just the shell of a team that we took over; it had been left in a pretty bad state. George Fury was our lead driver and I gave Glenn his chance in the ATCC as the second driver in a new Peter Jackson-sponsored Nissan Skyline DR30.

Once the team was up and running properly again, I started talking to Bo about finding another young guy to bring into the team. He told me I should have a look at this fellow Skaife. Once Bo had filled in some of Mark's background for me I decided to check him out. So I flew to Sydney one day – no-one knew I was doing this – grabbed a hire car, headed to Oran Park and stood in the crowd to see for myself what this rising star could do.

At that time there was a one-make Ford Laser Series for up-and-coming drivers. There were two Laser races at Oran Park that day; Mark took pole position for the first one and won it handsomely, then he ended up dead-set last at the start of the second and drove through the field and won that too.

Well, of course that made me sit up and pay attention. So I asked Mark's old man if his son would be interested in coming to Melbourne: no family, just the young fella. They were up for that, so down Mark came. No promise of a drive – we made it clear he was coming to us just to be part of the team in the first instance and we would see what happened.

Chris eventually found Glenn and Mark a place to live and of course it became a base from which they could cause havoc together! Throw in Anthony Tratt, another youngster who was a good mate of Mark and Glenn and living in Melbourne racing a Porsche – and let me tell you they created some dramas: the three of them terrorised the place.

An example: one time when I had just got home from Japan, Mark was most insistent we chat. He'd been racing Tratty – in road cars, on the streets – near the Nissan factory, and they'd had a crash. Mark was in a Nissan-owned vehicle, which was a problem in itself, especially since he had rolled the thing. The fibreglass briefcase that was his pride and joy – echoes of Ayrton Senna, I think – had not withstood the impact. It had burst open and his papers were everywhere. But the real problem was the copper in the bushes nearby with a radar gun checking speeds. That one took some smoothing over ...

We started using Mark for some test-driving, while Glenn took over the second car from Gary Scott. Skaifey didn't get to race really, because when I started to think I should do something for him we only had two cars. I talked Nissan into doing the 2.0 Litre Championship with one of their Gazelles for Mark to drive and he won that series easily.

But to me you are not a real race driver until you've competed in an open-wheel car. My own experience when I drove for Niel Allen showed me how much you can learn from those cars, and I was keen to get him into one. So we bought an English-built SPA for him to race in Formula Holden, which was briefly our local equivalent of the international F3000 series. In just his second year he won that title and then the next two for good measure.

Debriefing with Fred Gibson at Adelaide in 1988.

CHAPTER 3

GAINING MOMENTUM (THE GIBSON YEARS)

My years with Gibson Motorsport were amazing and did so much for my career. But first I had to endure two seasons of what felt like just watching before I finally got my chance to race full-time in the Australian Touring Car Championship. There'd been some cameos and I started with the Formula Holden, but I wanted to be an Australian Touring Car Champion and win Bathurst, and occasional drives in Skylines or Gazelles weren't going to do that. I had to wait for Godzilla – and we won a title in that before winning one in a Holden when they banned our car.

With Grant Jarrett racing the Gazelle in the 1987 Castrol 500 at Sandown. We finished 10th overall, the same position we'd finished in the same car at the Australian Touring Car Championship round held at the same circuit earlier in the year.

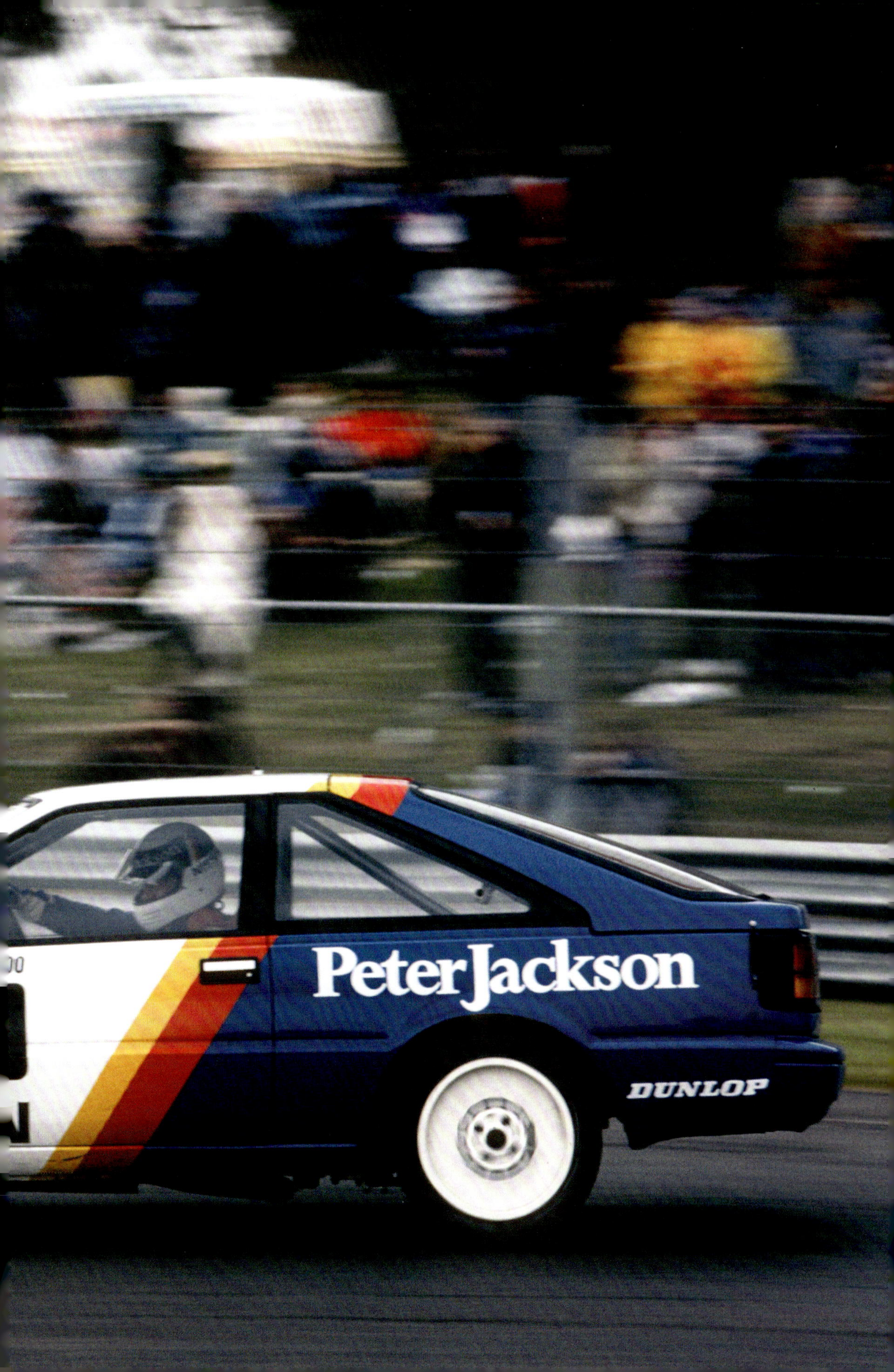
PeterJackson
DUNLOP

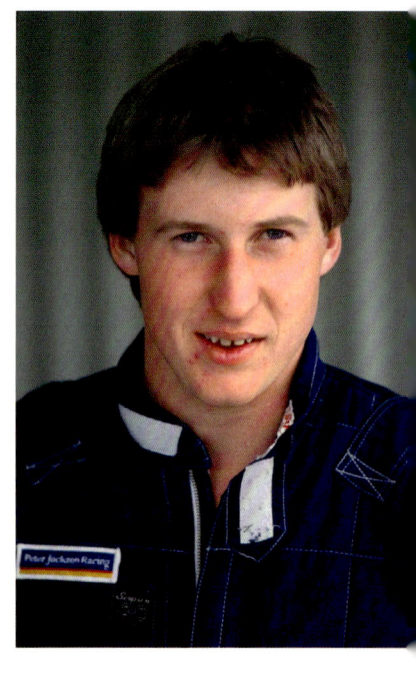

I finished 10th overall in my Australian Touring Car Championship debut at Sandown in 1987. This Nissan Gazelle was only a 2.0 litre class car, however it out-performed a range of bigger cars with more experienced drivers.

46   MARK SKAIFE

LEARNING LESSONS … AND PATIENCE

My early career was a difficult phase for a young bloke hungry to compete. I got a few test drives in the Skyline at places like Calder Park, but that wasn't enough, and neither was racing the Gazelle in the 1987 2.0 Litre Championship and at Bathurst.

The Gazelle was a great little car though. A Nissan dealer named Grant Jarrett was the push behind that. I won the 1987 Australian 2.0 Litre Touring Car Championship, which took place over four rounds. I won three of them, which was pretty good considering the effort Toyota was putting in with three cars and some pretty serious drivers. I also got my first points in the main Championship in that car because the Sandown round was also part of it.

A couple of other races were fun too, like the final running of the Amaroo Park 300. It was pissing down in the warm-up and I think it rained for the whole race that day. I was sharing with Terry Shiel, and in that warm-up I was the second-fastest car behind Jim Richards in a BMW M3. Terry crashed out of the race when he hit Steve Reed, who had stopped in the middle of the track on the exit to Dunlop Loop.

Everyone rated Jim in the rain, and he was colloquially known as the 'rain master', but we were second-fastest to him in a 'class' car. I thought I was making all the right noises, but with George Fury and Glenn driving the main cars I knew I'd have to wait.

Bathurst was interesting: it was part of the World Touring Car Championship that year and the best guys in the world were there with the best cars. Grant couldn't get the qualifying time required to start the race, so I had to go out with his helmet on to get him, and me, into the race. We broke the rules to get in and then the car overheated before the start and stopped on lap one. We lost a bucketload of time, but once we got running I did heaps of laps and it all contributed to my learning.

In 1988 I didn't race anything on a regular basis, but then the team didn't get the new cars on track until partway through the season anyway. Once the Ford Sierras arrived, it was just a waste of time running the old car, and there were so many delays out of Japan on the new HR31 and when it finally arrived it was unreliable and slow. I did the endurance races with George but that was a disaster, with DNFs at both Sandown and Bathurst. The only highlight at the end of 1988 was that Glenn and I ended up being the two fastest cars in the rain at Sandown.

In practice at Bathurst I had a crash too. I was chasing Alan Jones, who was driving a Caltex Sierra with Colin Bond, and I was sticking with him over the top of the Mountain. When we came out of The Dipper, Bruce Williams let Alan through but obviously didn't see me and turned in on me. I had the choice of hitting either the wall or him, so I chose him. He spun and I ended up spinning too and hit the wall anyway. I was feral.

It was a bit of a lesson for me. Both Fred and then John French – who was a mate of Fred's – said to me, 'You've got to be able to see if they can see you or not.' This comes from watching the driver's head move to check whether they caught you in the mirror. It was a pretty valuable lesson.

I had hoped the door would open when Glenn left the team to set up his own operation at the end of 1988, but Fred employed Jim Richards – and given I reckon he was the best touring car driver in the world at the time, it was a bit hard to argue. It turned out to be a game-changer for us, and me in particular, even though I didn't know it at the time.

A triumphant tipple after racing in the 1987 2.0 Litre Touring Car Championship at Winton, Victoria. The smaller cars had their own championship in that year, which I ended up winning after a season-long battle with the factory Toyota team.

OLLIE'S
AMILY RESTAURANTS
THE PRIME NETWORK
GO
GAZELLE
60
NISSAN
NISSAN FINANCE
NISSAN

Battling Toyota racer Drew Price in the opening round of the 2.0 Litre Touring Car Championship at Winton in 1987, where I finished third.

The Gazelle winning the 2.0 Litre Championship in the wet at Amaroo Park in 1987. It was a great car to learn in and it served its purpose.

52 MARK SKAIFE

Above: 1987 pit lane with Dad helping to push the Gazelle back into the garage.

Right: Out the back of the pits at Sandown with Glenn Seton and Dad in 1987.

GAINING MOMENTUM 53

WHEN DAD AND I LEFT NISSAN
Words by Glenn Seton, Australian racing driver and childhood friend

Dad and I moved to Melbourne in 1985 to join the Nissan racing team, and when we were down there Fred spoke to my dad about getting another young guy down into the team. Dad put Mark's name forward and Fred went and watched him race. Mark moved down to Melbourne to join the team and he lived with us for six months. Eventually he got his own place, but we were again spending a lot of time together both at work and socialising. That was the way it was until Dad and I left to set up our own team and we sort of went two separate ways for a while there.

Naturally Mark wasn't that happy about us moving on from Nissan, and our personal relationship was strained for a while. It took some time to get it back to near where it used to be. For a good three years, it was a 'hello' in passing and we were always amicable, but it was strained and unusual.

I'm not sure we ever had any big arguments from our racing, if we had something happen on the track we kind of made our points and then accepted each other's view and moved on – and that is how it has been forever. He probably could have sprayed me for the Fred situation and leaving Nissan Motorsport, but he never ever did.

Top left: Glenn and me in the workshop building Nissan HR31s during its development.

Top right: In 1988 with Dad; one of my best mates Anthony Tratt; my sister, Lisa, on the left; and my girlfriend at the time, Stacey, on the right.

Bottom: With another of my closest mates, Neil Crompton, at Oran Park in 1988.

GAINING MOMENTUM 55

My first proper Australian Touring Car Championship race in 1988, coming over the dogleg at Oran Park. It was the first time during the season we had run two cars, and I finished 12th.

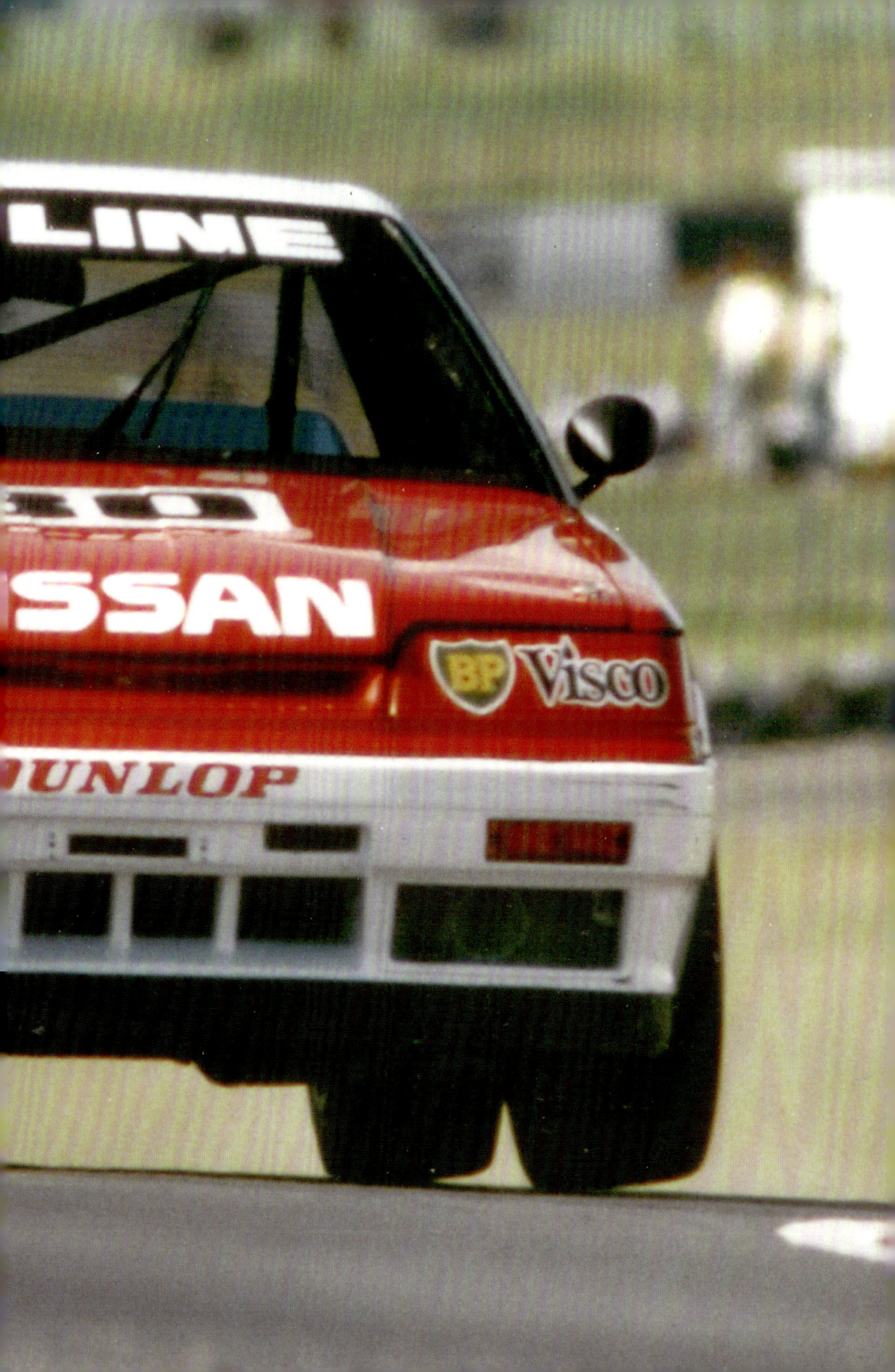
LINE
SSAN
BP
Visco
DUNLOP

JIM MADE IT LOOK EASY

I was pretty upset with Glenn and Barry Seton for leaving the team and taking the main sponsor with them, and we didn't really speak for a very long time. I felt like it was disloyal. Obviously they had been working on the deal for a while, but I have a bit more knowledge now and while I am still not a fan of it, I do understand.

We obviously had a fight on our hands to get the new HR31 up to speed in 1989, and that's where Jim Richards came into it. Man, you've never seen a bloke harder on a car than him; I can tell you he was no gentleman to the machinery. I remember our first day of testing with him at Winton. Fred basically said to us, 'You just drive the car as hard as you can possibly drive it, and we'll fix whatever the drama is.'

It went to a whole new level as soon as you added Jim Richards to that equation because he just attacked everything. He just drove the car harder and better than anybody I've ever seen. My god, he was good. I loved watching him drive; he seemed to have so much time on his hands that he made it look easy, but you couldn't see from the outside that he was torturing every single facet of the car.

Over the off-season we did a few test days, and there was one at Amaroo Park that was interesting for me. It was unbelievably hot and we were there for a couple of days. I did a best lap of 52.3 from my handful of laps, and Jimmy, who basically had all day, also did a 52.3. I knew on a track like that I wasn't too far away from him – I just had to keep working on the parts of my driving I needed to improve and learn other tracks that intimately.

When you applied the pressure of the race meeting, and having to do a lap at a certain time, Jim came into his own. He made us all look pretty ordinary and I knew I wasn't there yet. In that season we ran a third car for me at some rounds and I did Bathurst with Jim. It was the fast stuff I couldn't touch him on – remember, there was no data back then, so I couldn't compare traces or anything – but Jim was terrific, and he shared everything and answered my every question. He never hid anything from me, and when data came on it was evident that he hadn't been lying.

Top: On my way to my first Australian Touring Car Championship podium finish at Winton in 1989 aboard the factory Nissan Skyline GTS-R that I shared with Jim Richards.

Bottom: Jim Richards and I join Seven Network's Garry Wilkinson on the podium at Bathurst in 1989. Our Nissan finished third – this was my first Bathurst podium finish.

GAINING MOMENTUM

On the podium at Winton in 1989. I finished third behind Nissan teammate George Fury and Peter Brock.

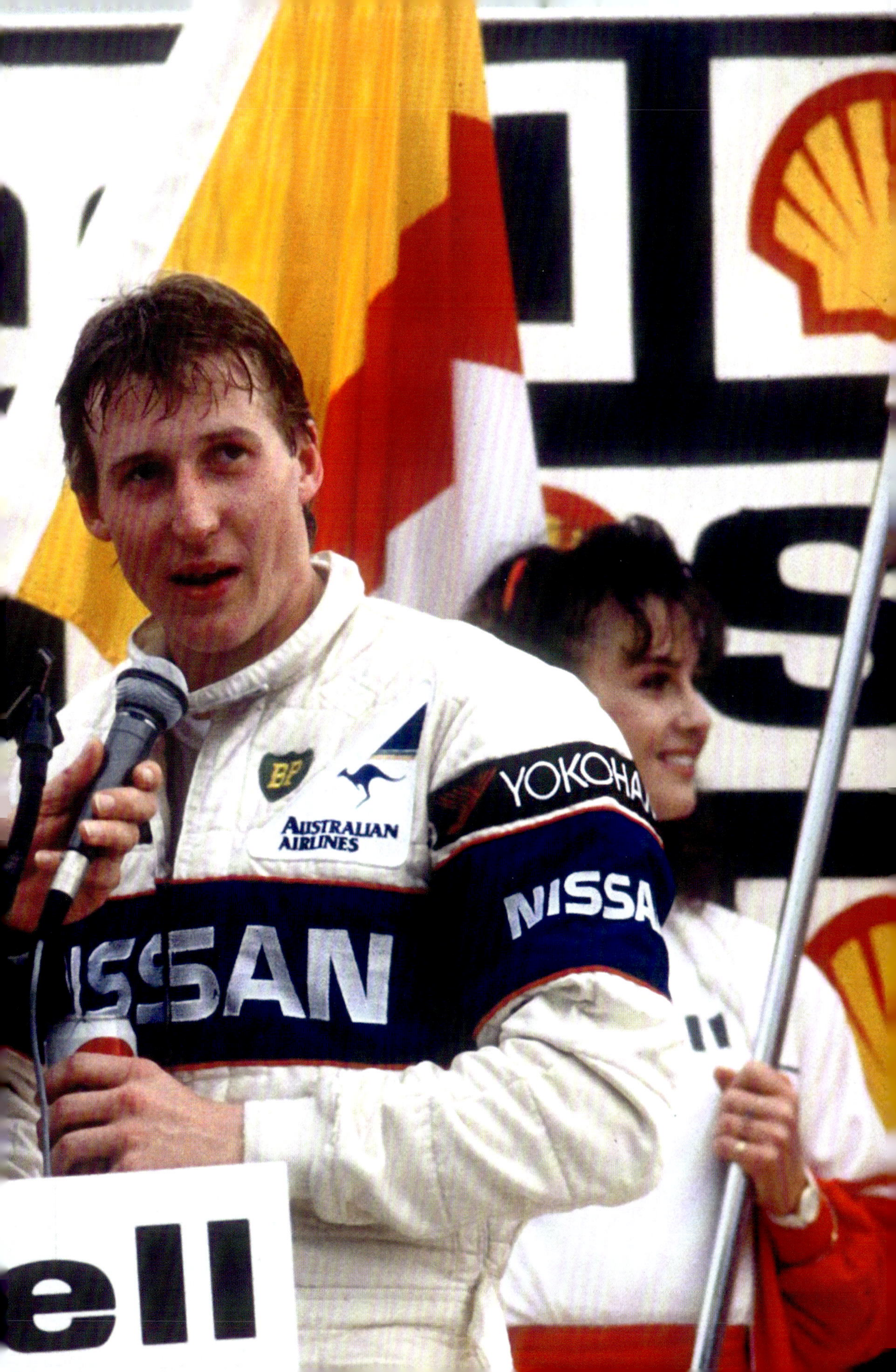

BP
AUSTRALIAN
AIRLINES
YOKOHA
NISSA
NISSAN
ell

I was learning as much as I possibly could in all areas of racing, whether it was technically or from a pure driver perspective. That Sandown 500 win with Jim was a highlight. There I was on pace with him, but at Bathurst I was still probably a bit more than a second a lap slower than Jim and I had no idea where or why. I didn't know where he was getting the time, so we'd talk and that would help, but I knew I had so much to learn – and that just made me hungrier to get in the car.

In late 1989 we'd seen the GT-R and started planning to roll it out here, and that meant that for me, 1990 was going to be another strange year.

Jim Richards and I share a Sandown 500 win in 1989.

THAT FATEFUL PAIRING
Words by Jim Richards, Kiwi racing driver and former teammate

I didn't know Mark that well until I joined the team. I'd seen him running in the little Gazelle and earlier on in the one-make Laser Series. I saw him start at the back of the grid in a Laser race and he ended up winning the race – he definitely had talent. There was a succession plan in place I think for him to replace George Fury, but after Glenn suddenly left the team those plans were shelved when they brought me in.

Glenn leaving wasn't just about a driver; he was taking the Peter Jackson money with him too, and I think the team needed to make a statement to Nissan and other sponsors that it didn't matter. We had a bloke who'd won championships and Bathursts before. They needed a lead driver, you might say. Not that it meant I was treated any better, by the way. Skaife got to run with me at Bathurst and he took over the second car the following year to replace George, so in reality it was just a slight delay in the plans.

When I got to see him up closer I saw a little bit more and got to see him grow quickly. When I told Fred I'd drive for him, the first thing he said we had to do was get me to drive the car. We went to Winton, and Skaifey, who did a lot of testing in the car, took it out and warmed it up with a few laps to make sure it was all okay. He did those laps and set a time, then I got in and I just expected to be quicker than him. I was a more experienced driver and I had been around a bit longer … But it was hard work trying to get down to his lap time. If I had thought he was good before, now I knew he was a bloody good driver.

He continued to get better too, which was great for the team and it didn't faze me one bit. I joined Nissan at a time when it needed to win a championship and win races, and we managed to do that for them. Mark did most of the testing and he was really good at that, and I was always happy to tell him anything, where I think some guys might have held back. I was never worried about Mark beating me. I knew that eventually he would because things were changing in the world of motorsport, where data and onboard computers and everything were coming into it, and I wasn't brought up in that era.

When data properly came into the sport, I used to look at Mark's lap then look at mine and see where I was slower or faster – then just work on those two corners or whatever. Whereas Mark would really get into the nitty gritty of honing the cars to get every last fraction of a second out of them. All I knew was that a car felt good and it was the way I liked to drive it. That was good enough for me, but it was never enough for him.

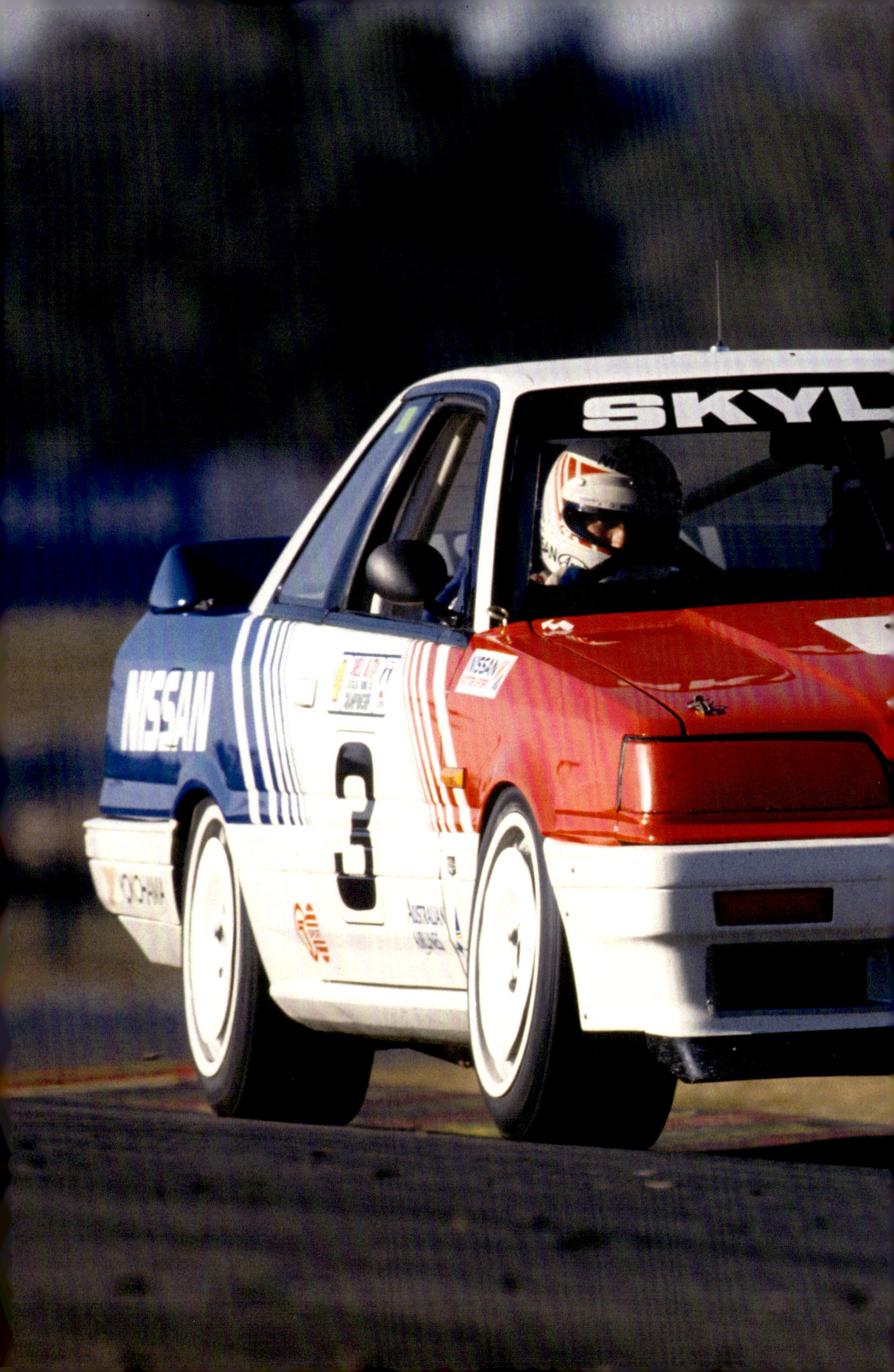
SKYL
NISSAN
3

Launching over the dogleg at Oran Park, Sydney, in 1990 aboard my Nissan Skyline GTS-R. By this stage we felt the GT-R – dubbed 'Godzilla' – was reliable enough for Jim to use it to wrap up the Australian Touring Car Championship, and I had to go back to the old car.

THE GUINEA PIG
Words by Fred Gibson, Australian racing driver and race team owner

Once we put Mark together with Jim Richards, he simply took off. Jim wasn't a good test driver, and what's more he hated doing it, but Mark was; Jimmy called him 'the guinea pig' because we would always get Mark to try something out on his car to see if it worked before putting it on his own. The two of them became good mates and that relationship helped Mark no end. He'd been doing similar data work with Ross Holder in Formula Holden, and when we got our hands on the GT-Rs his ability in that area was critical.

The GT-R was so advanced technically, we needed to grow quickly as a team, and Mark simply thrived – he loved it. We developed the best GT-Rs anywhere in the world – they were so good Nissan didn't want us to race them anywhere but Australia, even though we had plenty of offers to compete at places like Fuji. Kakimoto-san, who ran Nismo, blocked them all because he didn't want us to show up the locals. So we stayed domestic.

When it came to changing to Ford or Holden, that was a big move for us and we were competitive right from the start. But once we started to build the car the way we wanted we were setting the pace, and the Championship win in 1994 was very satisfying for all of us. But only a year or two after that, cigarette sponsorship was banned and we struggled to replace that funding.

Mark showed his true colours then. He was so loyal I virtually had to order him to take the HRT offer that came his way. He was part of our family; he'd grown so much with us that we didn't want to see it stop because of some sort of misplaced loyalty, admirable as it was.

Aside from his driving, he had also developed a great understanding of the whole business of motorsport. We were a team of people and he wasn't just one of our drivers. We were on the board of TCI (Touring Cars International) back in those days and Mark used to represent us there with people like Larry Perkins, Allan Moffat and Dick Johnson. He did sponsor pitches, worked on the special vehicles program when we were doing that for Nissan ... he was involved and totally invested in us. I knew it wasn't going to be easy for him to leave, but he needed to and we made sure that he understood that.

Summing him up, I would have to say that in some ways, Mark's not a natural driver. But he's a driver who will get the job done under any circumstances. What he and Richo did in the Nissan in the wet at Bathurst in 1992 was just unbelievable. Even though the GT-R was four-wheel-drive it was still not an easy car to drive in the rain, and in those conditions at his age he did a super job.

But that was Mark, and he was always the same. You put him in the car, he'd ask what he had to do, I'd tell him, and he'd say, 'That's gonna be hard', then he'd go out and do it. We had some great times together. Looking at where he is now and everything that he's done in his life, I have to say he's done a bloody good job. And he still talks as fast as he drove …

Tackling the Dunlop Loop at Amaroo Park, Sydney, in 1990 in my Nissan Skyline HR31.

TIMING, THE OLD WAY

In the days before data and proper timing, you still wanted to know what was happening with qualifying times and lap times during the endurance races. The big teams, like us, had a group of people just working stopwatches and recording data.

We had Chrissie and Margi, George Fury's wife, on the back of a ute, or wherever they could see from in pit lane, pushing buttons on maybe 10 stopwatches – one for each car we wanted to follow – inside a briefcase. They'd write down the times during practice and qualifying. When a session finished, you headed to that team to find out what had happened. In the races, we'd have someone yelling car numbers as they went past so Chrissie and Margi could keep a lap chart.

It seems mad today, but that's the way it was back then.

For my analytical mind, this was never going to be enough, so when data logging and other measures came into play that was right up my alley. We were the first team to have proper data, and with what I was learning in the Formula Holden that analytical ability remained a strength of mine to my very last race.

Margi Fury (centre) with Christine Gibson just behind her, timing us from the back of the Nissan Ute at Amaroo Park.

GAINING MOMENTUM 69

THE CAR NAMED GODZILLA

The change from the HR31 to the R32, or the Godzilla car as it became known thanks to a journo in Australia, made 1990 quite a complex year. When that car arrived, we knew that it was going to be a game changer like the BMW M3 or the Ford Sierra had been previously. But we also knew it wasn't going to be easy.

The Japanese, from a core technology perspective, had done a very good job of creating an absolute weapon. But from an execution point of view, it was terrible. The cars were fragile and there were such strange design choices, so while they were fast we struggled to keep them running. We knew we had to start building bits ourselves – and not just for the quality: a turbo was $38,000 alone, and it was a twin turbo, so you could imagine the bill there if we didn't do our own!

What really transpired was the 'Australianisation' of the car, and we did everything … new uprights, gearbox (we partnered with Larry Perkins to have a Hollinger box designed and built), the turbos. We even made our own wheels. It was a huge exercise but also the only way we could do it within the budget we had. Ultimately, we did the best job on that car of anyone globally.

We first ran the R32 in a test at Winton, and we knew we could do great things with that car. It was so complex for the time; we even had to program the four-wheel drive system. We were able to have four different modes in order to change that for wet or dry or for other balance requirements. I can't emphasise enough just how much work we did in that timeframe to get those cars up and going. It was just a remarkable engineering project.

I learned 100% the value of having not just good people, but the *right* people for the task. It showed me that there was a multitude of engineering strains, and that an engineer wasn't just an engineer. Kevin Drage from CSA did the wheels with us. Andrew Bartley did a stack of work on the uprights. Ross Holder was doing work on the electronics with the PI system, which logged data. We were the first ones with access to that that sort of system – we were actually the Australian agents – so we were pioneering data in this country. By the end of the project, we could drive the R32 as hard as an HR31, and we certainly couldn't do that at the start.

We debuted the GT-R at Bathurst in 1990 with Jimmy's Number 1 on the door, but it was still a little too fragile for a demanding race like that and we finished 15 laps off the lead. By Bathurst the following year (pictured), we were able to get the win.

GAINING MOMENTUM 71

Bathurst 1990: lifting the front wheel of the Nissan GT-R off the ground at Murrays Corner with a pack of Ford Sierras and Holden Commodores chasing. The race was my fourth Bathurst 1000 start.

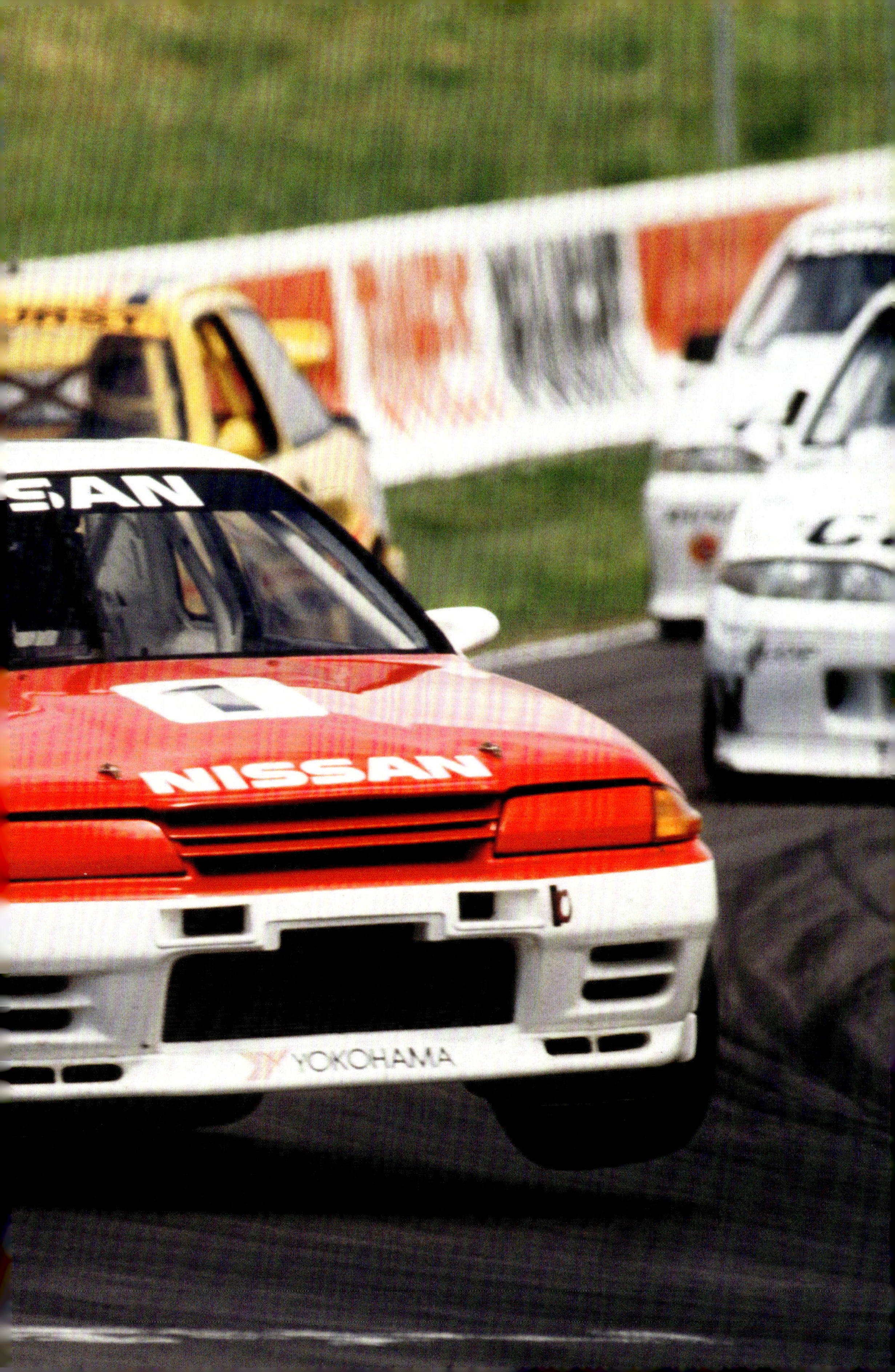
SAN
NISSAN
YOKOHAMA

I got one lap in qualifying the weekend we first rolled it out for a race at Mallala and put it on the second row on the grid. Jimmy was in Championship contention, so Fred decided that I'd run it first based on the massive technical challenges, and he felt it was too big a risk to Jim's title chances. We'd had all sorts of dramas: I hadn't even bedded brakes when I went out for qualifying, so I had to be very careful … I only had one lap to get on the grid. The second row was better than we expected.

If you watch the footage of the race on YouTube, you'll see how hard I had to work in that race. There are locking wheels, power slides and the whole lot – and passing Brock for the lead was far from easy. He had plenty of straight-line speed and I had to adjust my thinking. We'd come off the corners so well that if I was too close I'd have had to lift off. It took a while to work all of that out, then eventually I got through. I was still leading when the left-hand front hub broke, and that was a sensational effort on debut.

We knew the potential of what we had. Nissan had taken the rules of the class and built the ultimate car, but it was up to us to get it right for our conditions. It was a really cool time from there – step-by-step: break, analyse, fix, replace. It was so complex and advanced, even the suspension was way up there. If we fast-forward to the end of the GT-R program, when we had to switch ourselves into Holdens, we seriously just looked at all those blokes like they were kidding themselves because it meant we had to take such a backwards step in technology.

But we had to get through the two-and-a-half years we had with the car getting nobbled regularly and held back because people thought we had a bigger tennis racket. I was also getting wound up about people not crediting me with driving okay too; it might have been a good car but it wasn't easy to drive. Jim and I were also trying to beat each other, so we were driving the car as hard as we possibly could. Even silly things like jumping in Mark Gibbs's GIO GT-R sometimes was an eye opener, because the Dunlop tyre was sometimes actually faster than the Yokohama we were using, so we could have been even better.

Right: Godzilla was fast in its Bathurst debut in 1990. Here I'm watching on as the Nissan team gets to work.

Left: Yours truly, left, and Fred Gibson, right, in conversation with then-Nissan Australia Chairman and Managing Director Ivan Deveson in pit lane at Bathurst in 1990.

GAINING MOMENTUM 75

THE BIGGEST CRASH OF MY LIFE

At Adelaide in the 1990 Grand Prix support race, I had a huge crash. Richo and I were battling for pole position and it was my first lap in qualifying. We now had the PI System data logger in the cars so we could look and get measurements around what was happening. Importantly we could find out exactly what the car was doing at any given part of the lap. I knew I was getting big gains on Jimmy coming on to the back straight, which was onto Dequetteville Terrace, a really fast right-hander where Mika Häkkinen had his big crash a few years later.

It was a great corner, a really fast fourth-gear corner that is a little bit like turn eight now, but slower. It had a big kerb on the inside and a massive kerb on the outside, and I remember driving up over it in practice and knew I could get away with it, no problem. So I blazed in there, turned it in and slid towards the outside kerb, but the turn had a bit more force in it than on other laps because it was on new tyres and it was pretty wild. When I hit the kerb, it broke a wheel; the car turned straight over on its roof and was still going fast. I remember turning down to try and stop the car from turning over, but it didn't really work. No matter how hard I pressed the brake pedal, it just wouldn't slow down.

Man, it hit hard.

As it was running towards the fence on its lid, the road ground its way through the top of the A pillar and the roof and into my helmet. So it got grazes all over it and it flattened a big section of my helmet as it was heading towards the fence. When it hit, oh man, it bounced back right back into the middle of the track and it was rotating on its roof, and they couldn't get me out because the door was so damaged. A heap of guys pulled up, like Joe Sommariva who was driving a BMW 635, Colin Bond and I think Peter Brock too. But when I was stuck in there the marshals were yelling out, 'Fire! Fire!' God, it wasn't getting any better. I was stuck in there and she was going to light up. It was just unbelievably frightening.

No-one knows this, but I actually damaged my left eye in the crash and I was so sore I lay in a Nissan Patrol the whole of the next day. I went to the medical centre, I was chewing Panadol Fortes like Smarties and I've never been in so much pain in my life. It was really hot over in Adelaide that time of year and I just lay there in the Patrol with the air conditioner on; I couldn't move. I kept blinking all the time and there was a fuzzy spot in my eye. If you've ever been knocked out you'd remember all those little fuzzy spots that go into your vision – it was like they were all compacted together in one little spot, right in the middle of my eye.

I couldn't get my brain around what it was – it was very strange. So I went back to Melbourne and Christine Gibson took me to the hospital to have my neck and everything checked. We did all the MRI stuff and then the doctor said I should have all these others scans to see why my eye was funny.

Dr Kevin English, an ophthalmologist in Brisbane, had looked after a minor eye injury for me in the past, so I got on a plane and flew up to see him. He went through a whole host of checks and said I had scarred the retina with the impact. Everything in your head moves in a crash like that, and some of the movement had damaged my eye.

We never told anyone, though – we kept it quiet the whole time. Kevin said my eyes would find a work-around for it, and they have, but it is still there. My brain has rewired itself to make it a non-issue, but if I take the time to find it, I still can.

There was also some damage to the L5/L4 discs in my spine, which had been dislodged when my back was basically crushed. The roof had been pushed down and the seat wasn't moving, so something had to give, and the something was those discs in my back.

That crash was a real drama. I almost missed the next race meeting which was the Nissan 500 at Eastern Creek and Neil Crompton was drafted into driving with Jimmy just in case, but I arrived pretty late and got in the car and drove. It was obviously good to get back on the horse, but it was also very frightening because I didn't know how much the vision thing was going to hurt me. Fortunately, when I drove the car I was on the pace. But it was quite a nerve-wracking time. 🏁

1990 at Phillip Island was my first weekend with the SPA Formula Holden with Peter Schaefer and Harry Galloway helping me with the car.

Top and bottom right: 1990 was my second season in the Formula Holden and I won all bar one round to claim my first of three Australian Drivers' Championships.

Bottom left: 1991 at Eastern Creek with Peter Schaefer, Fred Gibson, Belinda, who was my wife at the time, and Rod Smith.

In my Nissan GT-R at Sandown in 1991.

CHAPTER 4

THE TURNING POINT

When I set goals I was brutal on myself about the consequences of missing my targets. As I have said before, I was hungry and I wanted to take it all on and win. But first I had to beat Jim Richards in the same car. To me, he was the yardstick and the best touring car driver in Australia, if not the world. I had my work cut out for me, but I knew if I could do that it would prove I was good enough. If not, I reckoned I should pack my bags and head home to the family business.

MAKE OR BREAK

I'd had glimpses at getting better and probably more consistent as a driver, and at some places I was just as fast as Jim. Not everywhere, mind you, but it started me thinking.

I was having a beer with Dad back in Wyong leading into the 1990 season and we were talking about how I thought the year ahead was going to be a make or break one. I said to Dad, 'If I can't beat Jim Richards, then I'll be coming home; I'm done.' That was about me recognising who was the best driver in the land, being his teammate, and being able to compete against him. If I couldn't do that, I was never going to be what I wanted to be. In my mind it was simple.

Dad was a bit confronted by the conversation because he thought that at my age – 23 at the time – I was being a bit harsh on myself and trying to fast-forward the process too much. I told him that wasn't the case, but I had to make a call on whether I could do this for a living and get somewhere with it.

I knew it was going to be one thing to match Jim's speed, to outqualify him, but another to beat him in races. I didn't know at that time how little racing we'd do in the same model car during the season, so I guess make or break shifted to a year later.

The first time I outqualified Jim on pure speed was at Lakeside in 1990, which I felt was significant because it was a hard track with severe consequences. The next year I got my first pole at Mallala and then I did it again a few weeks later at Lakeside.

It took a bit of a mental effort for the Lakeside pole. Jim said he was going through the left-hand kink flat, and I was lifting a bit so I had to talk myself into it. That was a wild corner. It wasn't just the shape of it; it also had a really big bump and it would pitch the car outside to the right and there were a lot of big crashes on the day. You'd be north of 230km/h in the kink in qualifying.

To get through there flat, we had the driver's side wheels on the inside of the white line along the edge of the track. The whole rest of the car was effectively on the grass flat out, then you'd bounce to the other side, holding your breath the whole time, and try to stop it for the next corner, the Carousel. That stretch of track was just great; that's exactly what car racing is about. You couldn't do a whole race like that, of course, but you still had to use the grass at quite a few spots to get the lap time. 🪖

My Nissan GT-R in action at Lakeside, Queensland, in the 1991 Australian Touring Car Championship. I finished second behind Jim Richards after starting on pole.

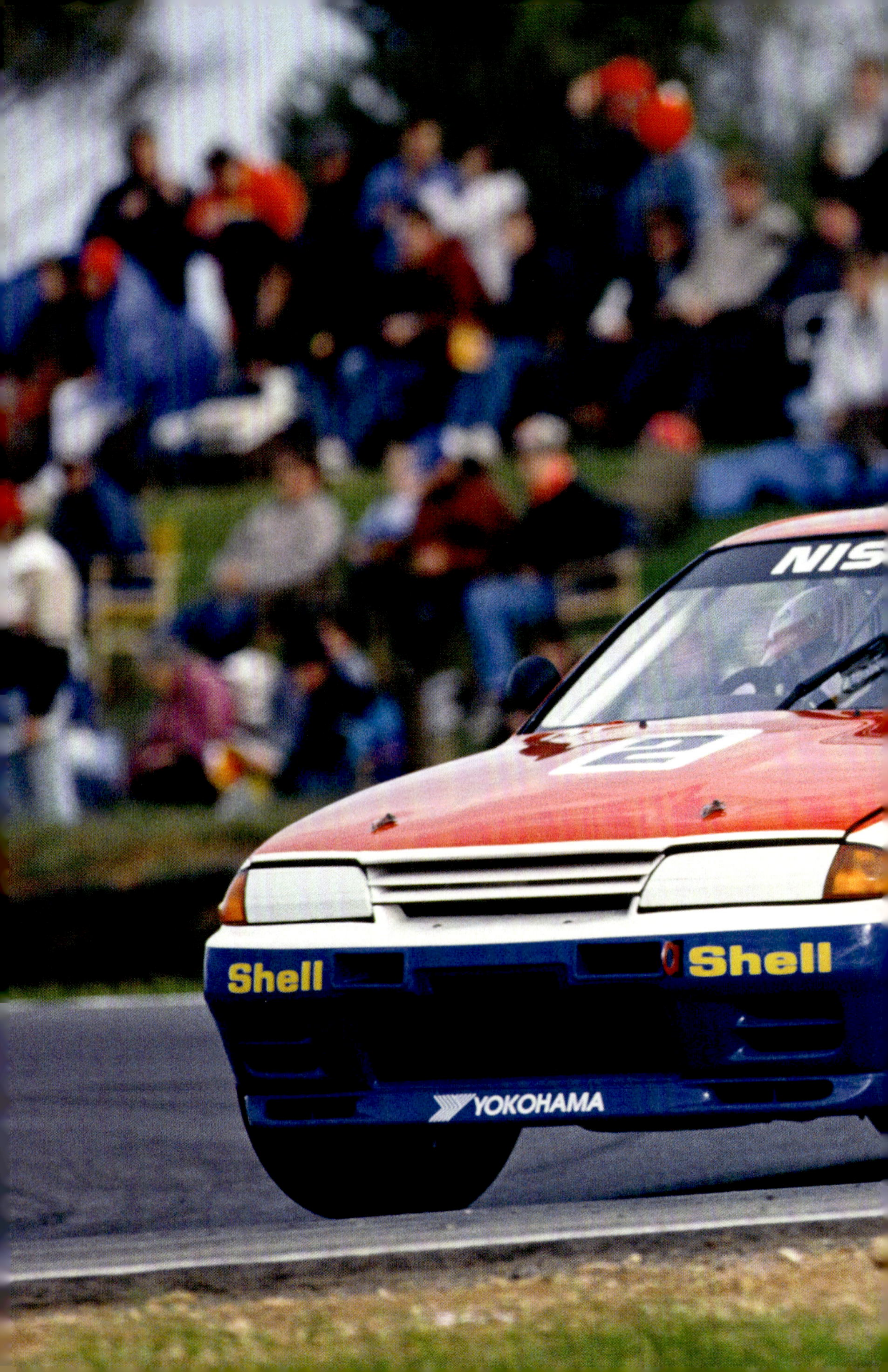
Shell
Shell
YOKOHAMA

I'd scored my first Australian Touring Car Championship win earlier in 1991 in Western Australia and I added to the tally at Mallala in South Australia. Here my Nissan tackles the hairpin at the end of the back straight.

THE MINDSET

I always figured that if someone else could do something in a car, I could too. Sometimes I just had to convince myself to do it. It's probably similar to the mad blokes who surf those big waves or people who jump out of aeroplanes – you have to take a leap of faith at some point or you'll never do it.

Qualifying, and that need for absolute commitment, is something that has always turned me on. I loved the opportunity to drive the car as hard as I could possibly drive it, right at the limit of having a crash, but without overstepping.

I loved shootouts. The really cool aspect of those is that there is a bit of a surprise element – you might not have been on the track for an hour or more, so you really wouldn't know how much grip there was going to be, where you could brake or how fast you could go through a corner.

You had to feel it on the warm-up lap. You had to use all your innate skill and intuition to process information, which feeds through all the senses on that one lap. No-one ever wants to crash, so there's a level of intellect that comes from understanding all those nuances and those circumstances – understanding what you might've done in the warm-up phase for that tyre, for instance, and how it translates to a full-speed run.

In a weird way we always talk about championships and race wins, but for me the purity of the sport is all about how fast you can do a lap. In Formula One there was the theatre of doing the pole lap just on the chequered flag, for instance, like Ayrton Senna. For us in many places, there was the thrill of doing it in a shootout as the last car and all the pressure that comes from that. I loved both the spectacle and the challenge.

But if you map that out over a career, I don't think the raw speed part changes; you've either got that or you don't. But your race craft evolves and you can become a better race driver – I knew that even back in 1991 when I beat Jim for pole. I had the speed, I just had to work out how to be a smarter, better race driver.

OUR FIRST BATHURST WIN TOGETHER
Words by Jim Richards, Kiwi racing driver and former teammate

When we won Bathurst together for the first time it was special to me for a number of reasons. I had the three wins with Brocky, but it was really his team and I was just a driver that came in a couple of times a year. I didn't feel much like a part of a team; in the four years I was with them I didn't spend much time there at all – just go up to Bathurst and win, but it felt like most of the drivers in pit lane could have done that.

In 1989 Mark and I finished on the podium, and with that car it was a great feeling. But in 1991 when we won the race, it felt more like I was part of something than I did with Brock. Winning it with Mark was even better, this was our third year together and we had built such a strong relationship even though I was the same age as his father. There was no big-headedness or ego involved, we just wanted to get our car as fast as we could and we both drove it as hard as we could.

Mark always wanted to change things. I just had to be honest with how I thought it felt. I had no idea what they changed or what they did, but Mark was great with that which meant we were perfect for each other. We drove as a team; if I couldn't win I would do all I could to help him win. If I was good enough, I'd beat him and if he was good enough he'd beat me and we felt that was the only way to move forward as a team. When we were together in the same car, it was different obviously, and I would have driven with him forever at Bathurst.

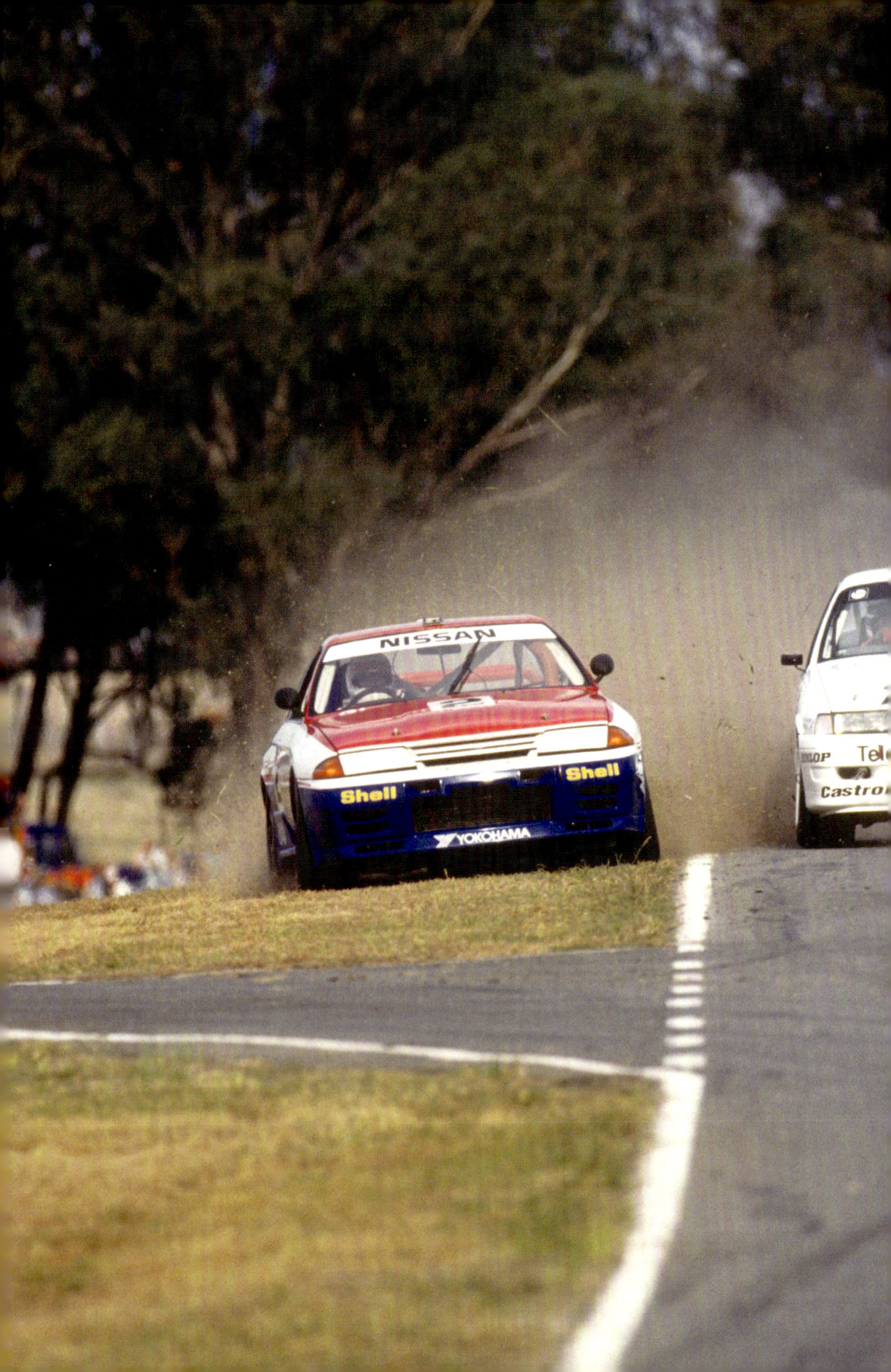
NISSAN
Shell
Shell
YOKOHAMA
Castro

This trip through the grass off the start line at Winton in 1991 earned me a pit lane stop-go penalty. But I still managed to finish second despite the delay.

PICKING UP SPEED

Jimmy and I had come out of the blocks fast in 1991. All the work on the GT-R in the back end of 1990 and over summer had given us a car that was reliable enough for us to drive hard. Jim was the reigning Champion, and I was keen to make my mark. At the time I had never to this date run a full Australian Touring Car Championship, and I was finally getting my chance.

Jim won the first two rounds of the 1991 Championship at Sandown and Symmons Plains, and then we went to Perth for the round at the track we now know as Barbagallo. It's a great track – I'd driven the GT-R there the previous year and it was, and is still, a real car-control track that I liked right from that first visit. It's a low-grip track and the cars slide around, which damages the tyres. It still has that tendency today and is the hardest place on tyres per kilometre in Australia. So often it felt like driving in the rain, but if you were able to make the tyres last while still going fast enough, there were big gains later in the races.

On this weekend, I was driving no better than Jim, but the cards fell right and I had my first ever round win – even though I'd run fewer than 20 rounds in my career to that date. I think in all Australian motorsport history up to that point, only around 20 people had actually won a round of the Championship. So that was pretty big in a 24-year-old's life.

Jim won the next two rounds, so we had won the first five rounds of the Championship before Tony Longhurst beat us in the BMW M3 at Amaroo Park. He also won at Lakeside, but I won the other two in the back half of the season. I actually finished the season with more points than Jim, but the crazy system at the time said you had to drop your worst score, which was a fourth place for me while Jim had a DNF at Oran Park – so he won the title while I won the round.

In 1990 I had started in the Australian Drivers' Championship, which Fred thought would help my overall driving and testing ability. I won a couple of rounds in my first season, but I dominated 1991, winning all but the first round, which Mark Larkham won. I felt like I was driving really well, and Fred was right about what I was learning. I was spending so much time in cars – whether it was the open-wheeler or the GT-R for tyre testing or whatever – that I was really making up for missing out in those early years with Fred.

Top: The Gibson Motorsport team tends to my high-tech, four-wheel-drive, turbocharged Nissan GT-R at Sandown in 1991. Team owner Fred Gibson is to the left of shot in discussion with Shell/Dick Johnson Racing team manager Neal Lowe.

Right: My first Shootout and pole at Bathurst, in 1991. It was an exhilarating lap. Jim Richards and I won in the GT-R that year, my first Bathurst win.

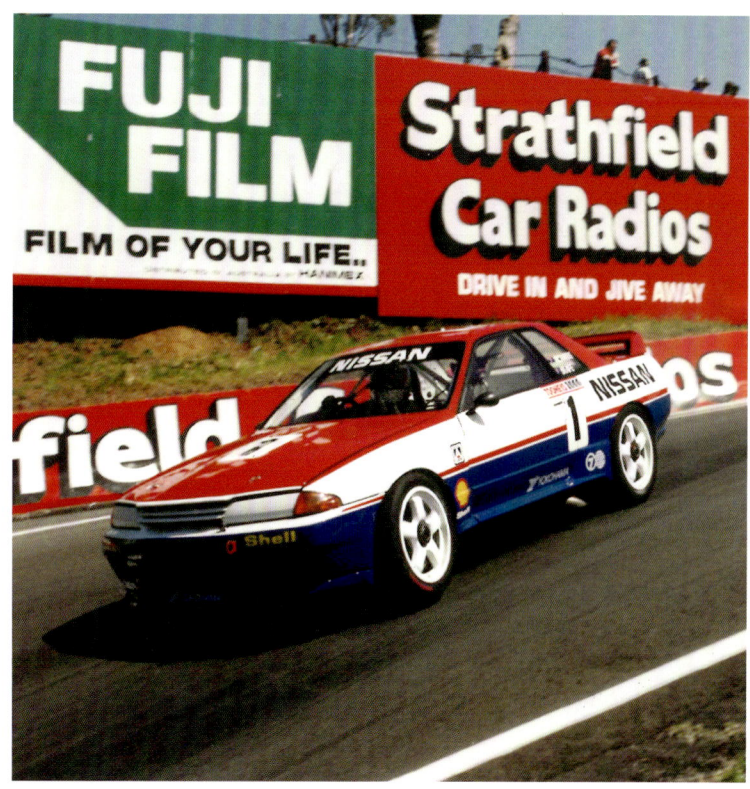

THE TURNING POINT 91

Celebrating the Bathurst win in 1991.

Top left: Dad and Mum with me and Brad Leach, who was the motorsport PR manager at Nissan.

Top right: Celebrating with Fred.

Below: Chrissie Gibson planting a kiss on me.

Top: Jim Richards and I meet the press after winning the 1991 Bathurst 1000. The win was my first in Australia's 'Great Race' and the first win by a Japanese car in the history of the event.

Left: What a feeling! Celebrating my first Bathurst 1000 win in 1991 with Nissan.

THE TURNING POINT 93

I won the final round of the 1991 Australian Touring Car Championship at Oran Park, Sydney. Here I've stopped on the slow down lap to give Jim Richards a ride back to the pits – Jim's car had failed mid-race with engine problems.

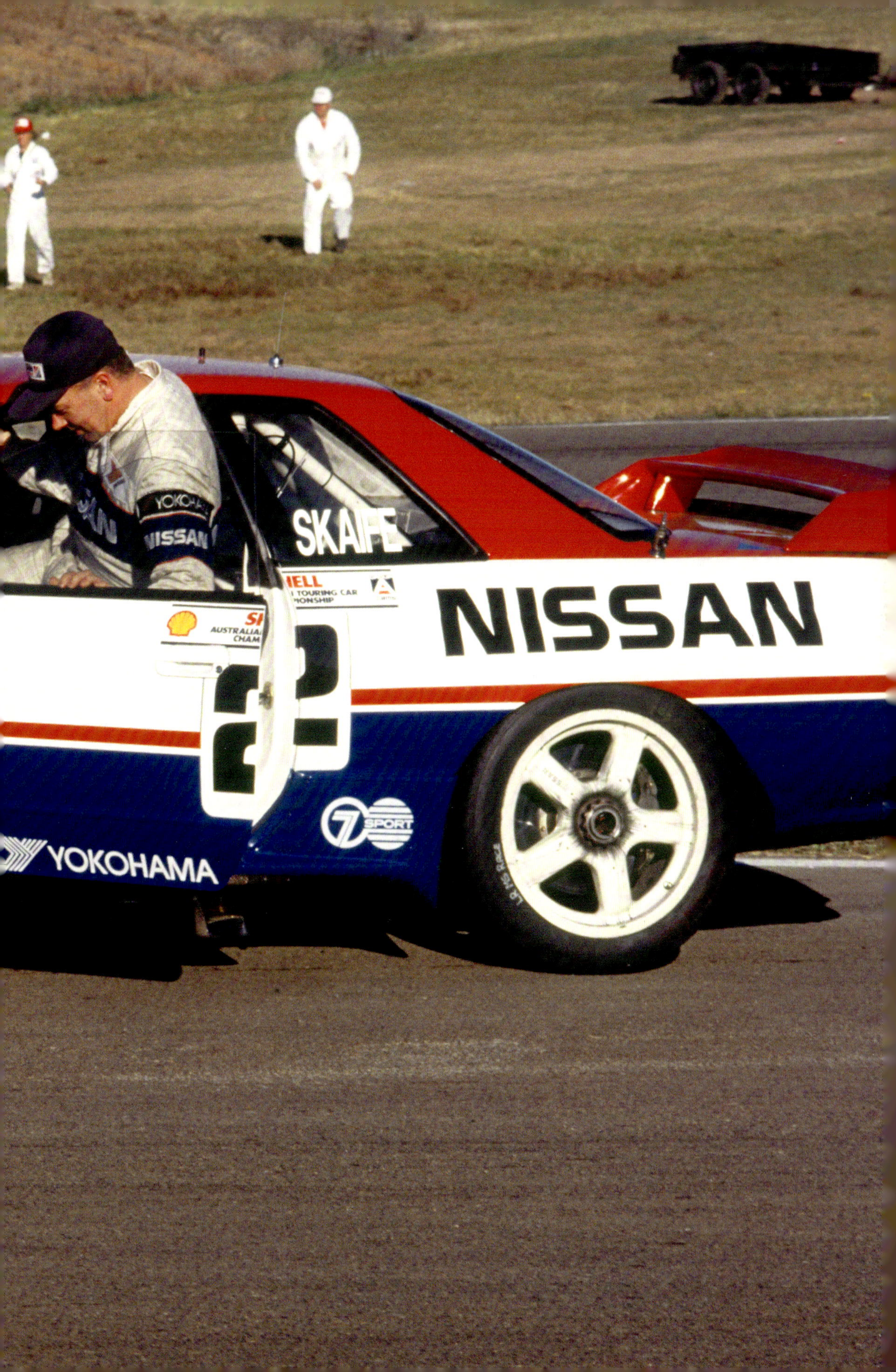
SKAIFE
NISSAN
YOKOHAMA
SPORT

THE YEAR OF 115 DAYS IN A RACE CAR

Fred always had the feeling that driving open-wheel cars improved your skill set – and he was absolutely right. When you drive purpose-built race cars, you can tune more things to your liking and you get to a stage where you demand more of the car. I suppose throughout my career that's been one of my trademarks – demanding more of the car and translating that into lap speed.

We entered a car in the Australian Drivers' Championship, which was being raced in what they called Formula Brabham and eventually Formula Holden. They were Formula 3000 chassis from Europe with a Holden V6 engine and they were fast. In terms of lap speed, they blitzed a touring car. As I developed greater technical skills, we were able to be more critical of the touring car, which helped its development. It made me feel like the touring car was a taxi; guys like Ross Holder and Andrew Bartley hated it when I'd get back in the touring car and complain about all its faults.

That was a really good part of my career, partly because I was running the road-car business on the side of the factory with two or three guys, which helped fund the open-wheeler effort in the race team. I learned a lot because in those days there were a few good operators in open-wheel land, but it was different to touring cars. I had two guys, Pete Schaefer and Scott Owen, as well as some mates of mine – Anthony Tratt, Rod Smith and open-wheeler specialist Harry Galloway – and a small crew of us that would go away, with Dad and Fred also helping when they could. We worked hard on running it cleanly and efficiently, which ultimately was successful for us.

I enjoyed those weekends. There wasn't as much politics and there wasn't as much media hype, which allowed me to concentrate on driving and working with that group of people as best as we could.

That was just at the time when data acquisition was taking off. Ross Holder, who was in our Nissan team, also started coming along to those weekends and we started lifting our professionalism and had a ripper time. There was good competition and there were some very good teams with strong funding. Mark Larkham with Mitre 10 was spending a bucketload of money; they were doing an excellent job. He had good people around him too – Greg 'Pee Wee' Siddle was running the program; Bruce Carey, who was a guru of the day; and a young Sam Michael, who ended up running Williams F1, was looking after the engineering.

We were already working hard before the open-wheeler program, but I can tell you we were just eating, sleeping and breathing motorsport. I calculated that in 1991 I spent 115 days in a racing car of some form, which was just incredible.

There were certainly times back then when there was a risk I could overload on motorsport – where motorsport was all-consuming, and perhaps it wasn't all that healthy. But you end up getting so caught up in your own little world that sometimes you don't see the forest for the trees.

It was a big thing for me: I'd moved to Melbourne at 19 not knowing anybody, really having to dedicate my life to working hard to get ahead. Five years later, we'd won Bathurst, the Drivers' Championship and the ATCC, and we were on the road and going alright … but I had to use all my energy, brainpower and effort to get to that point. I wasn't going to blow it by a half effort.

It took sacrifice – and that included my social life and other activities. There were certainly times when I would have loved to have gone to the footy or to have gone out and had a beer, or indulged in my other favourite passion: chasing sheilas – but it was pretty difficult to be a normal bloke with what I was doing.

I don't know if I could have worked harder or dedicated more of my energy to making a career in motorsport.

We won the Australian Drivers' Championship in 1991, 1992 and 1993. The final round for the 1992 season was at Oran Park, and I needed to win in both the open-wheeler and the touring car to win both championships. At that time no-one had ever won both titles, so to win both on the same day in the same year was pretty big.

Preparing to race at Eastern Creek in Sydney in 1994. By then I'd adopted the deep blue, red and yellow helmet colours that I'd carry for the rest of my racing career.

CHAPTER 5

A NEW ERA

I had a lot of options at the end of 1992, and to be honest I was pretty much over what was going on in Australia. The way the crowd responded to our Bathurst win that year was gutting, and we were lucky Jim said what he did – I wasn't going to be so nice about it. But it started a shitstorm I didn't want to be a part of. My Formula Holden campaign and championships meant I was thinking a little about whether I could race something like Formula 3000 in Europe, or maybe I could drop into a Nissan program somewhere. It didn't work out, but it sounded good at the time.

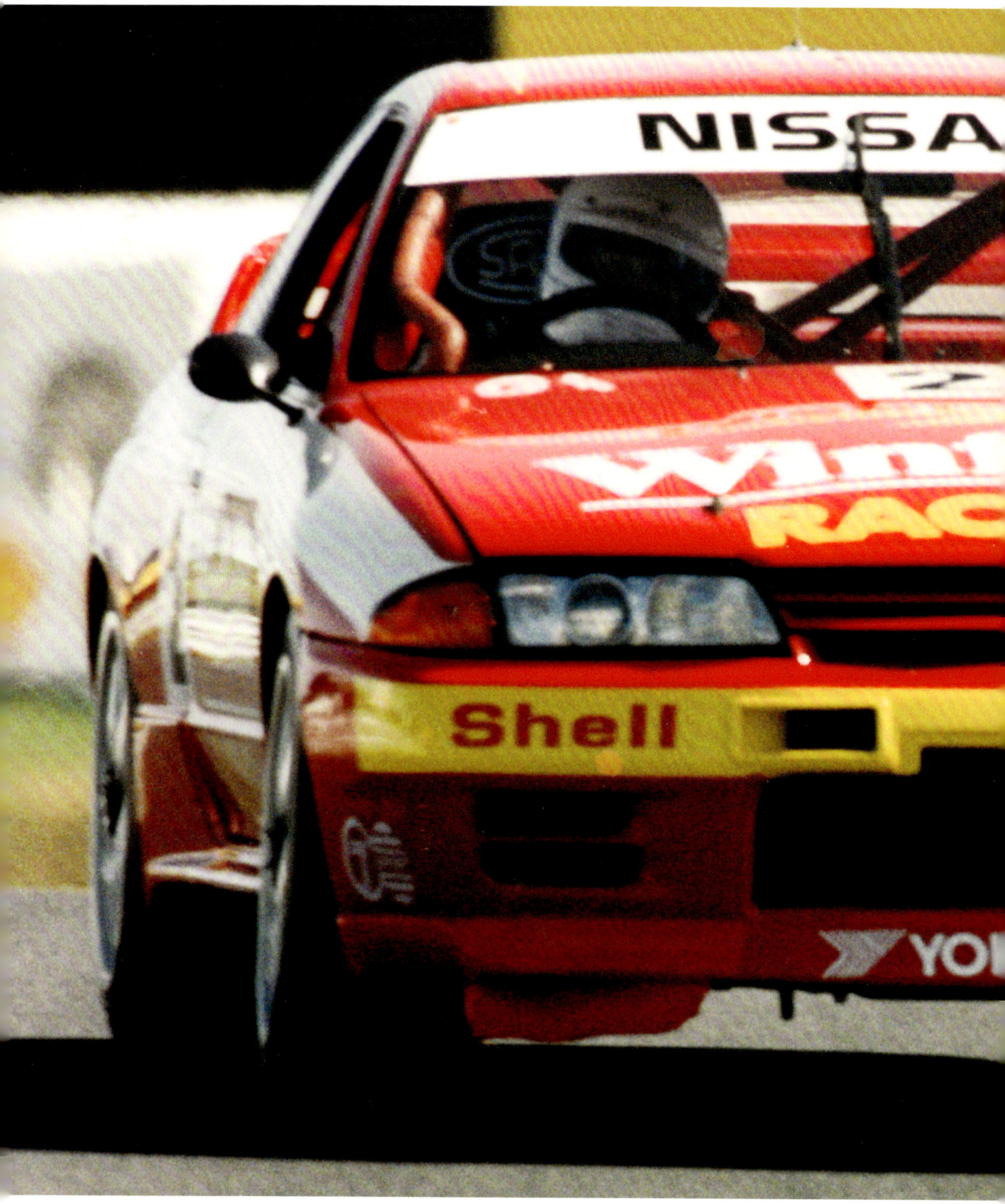
Shell

One of my favourite photos – this is the GT-R in full flight under the bridge at Lakeside in 1992. The car was significantly handicapped at that time and was bloody hard to drive.

THAT BATHURST

The 1992 Bathurst race is burned into my memory. Even though Jim and I secured the win, the race was fairly disastrous on a number of fronts.

It was one of the most treacherous days at Bathurst. Jim and I had been comfortably leading the group for the whole race, but the rain was just making the track impossible to drive on with any sort of speed or control – even in a car like Godzilla. That's another thing that didn't help our campaign: we were in a Nissan and the diehard Ford and Holden punters had their hearts set on us failing. More on that in a moment though.

The most tragic outcome of that particular race day was losing Denny Hulme, another driver (1967 Formula One World Champion) and friend of Jim's who suffered a fatal heart attack at the wheel. That's always a sobering thing to happen in a race and suffice to say emotions were running high.

There were rivers of water on Conrod Straight and one of them washed our car away when we were leading, taking us into a pile of other crashed cars. The race was red-flagged and I reckon Dick Johnson thought he'd secured the win. Jim and I were back in the pits when we learned that *we* were the actual winners, because when a race is red flagged, the winner is the leader on the lap before … and that was us.

We were chuffed; we knew we were the fastest car and that we'd put in the best drive that day, so it was devastating when the Holden and Ford fans booed us at the dais. I don't care to rehash that part in too much detail because I really don't think it reflects the spirit of the sport. I will say this though: despite all the fuss it caused, when Jim Richards called that crowd of hundreds a 'pack of …' – the video's still on YouTube somewhere if you want to relive the raw moment – he gifted us with an iconic moment in Australian motorsport history. As ever, I was grateful to have him by my side.

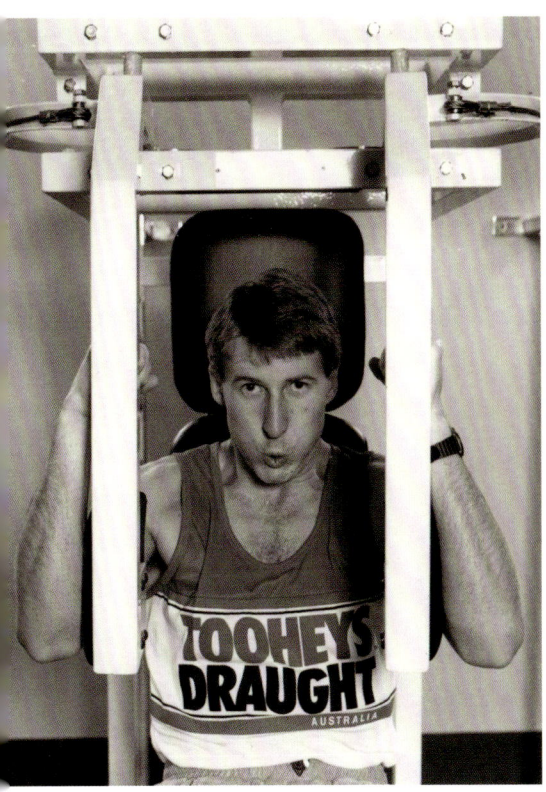

Top: On the grid ready for the start of the 1992 Bathurst 1000. Jim Richards and I won the race; the Nissan GT-R crashed in wet conditions later in the day but was awarded victory.

Left: The glamour shots come out – here I am, 'pumped up' for the Tooheys-sponsored Bathurst 1000 in the early 1990s.

A NEW ERA 103

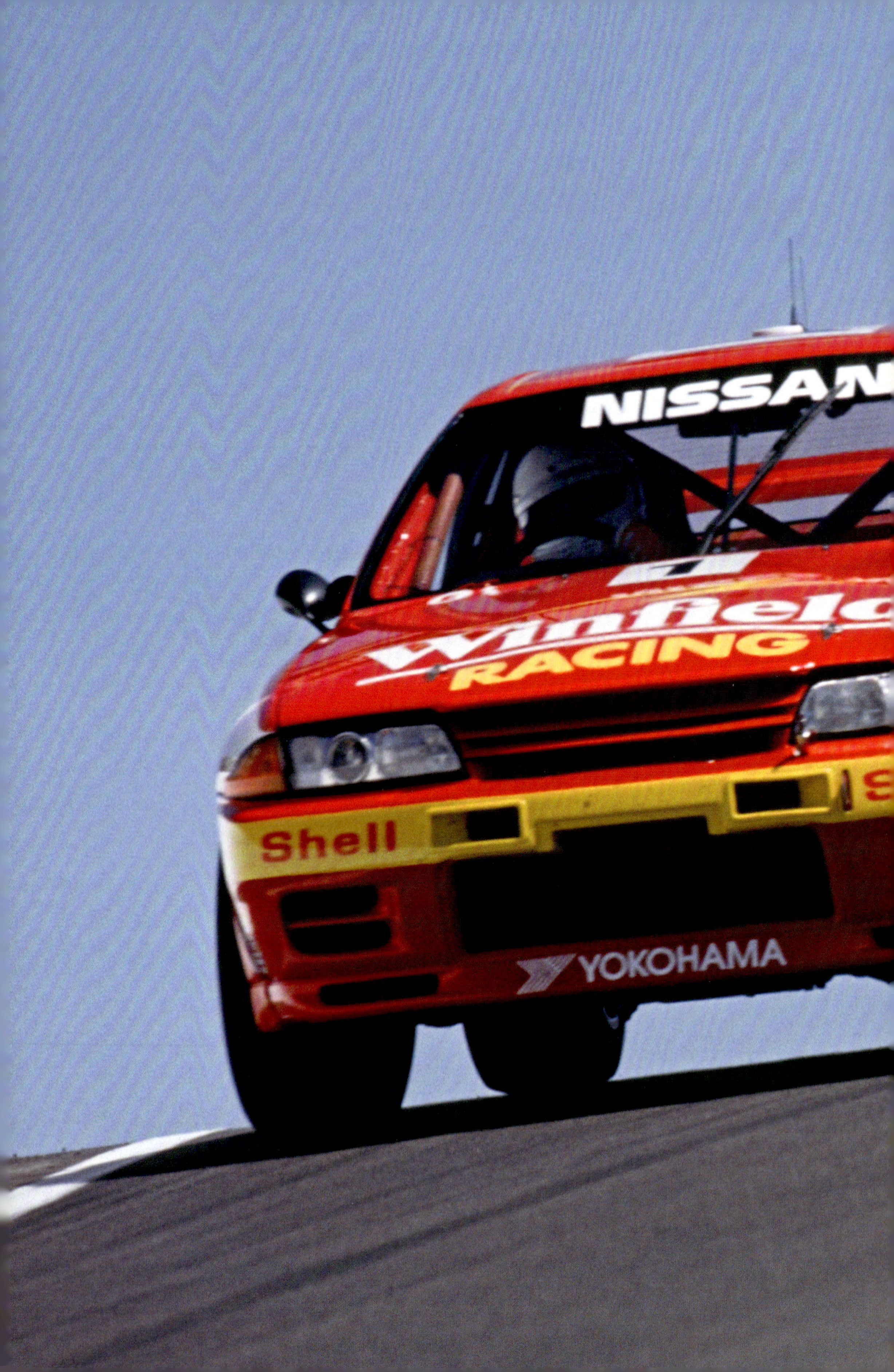
NISSAN
RACING
Shell
YOKOHAMA

Roaring across the top of Mount Panorama and negotiating what is now known as 'Brock's Skyline' on the tough Bathurst circuit. This is from the 1992 Great Race, though the blue sky behind indicates it's a shot from practice given race day was plagued by rain and overcast conditions.

Above: With Jim Richards celebrating winning the shortened Bathurst 1000 in 1992. Jim had crashed in wet conditions, though officials stopped the race and the results backdated to the last full completed lap. In this shot, we'd just received the news confirming our second straight Bathurst win.

Above: Jim Richards and I copped abuse from a hostile crowd when we stepped out onto the podium after being declared winners of a rain-shortened Bathurst in 1992. Jim is about to deliver his famous line while Michael Wesslink, Tooheys MD, and a soon to be gobsmacked Garry Wilkinson flank us on the podium.

A NEW ERA 107

QUELLE BLOODY *HORREUR*

I jetted off to France to do some Formula 3000 races right after that Bathurst in 1992, and with what was going on after that podium it wasn't such a bad thing to be away from it.

Jim's jab at the crowd had certainly started a storm, and the Ford and Holden camps were winding them all up and creating a frenzy. We felt like public enemy number one. Thankfully then, in the days before social media, you could really escape. So mentally I had no dramas putting it behind me, especially from all the way over in France.

I landed in France to drive a Reynard 92D Mugen Honda for 3001 International, which was run by Mike Earle, who had previously run Onyx Grand Prix. He was a really lovely guy and reminded me a lot of Fred Gibson actually, but money was pretty tight. Allan McNish, who had been driving the car, had run out of money and that opened the door for me. Hideki Noda was driving the team's other car and he had no points in the season, while Allan had a handful and a podium to show for his seven races.

Time was always tight, so whenever I went to Europe, I'd land at maybe five or six in the morning and then head to a track somewhere and drive. Sometimes you'd have changed flight somewhere, so you'd have spent a lot of time cooped up in a plane.

The Circuit Paul Ricard is in the south of France, just outside Marseilles in Le Castellat. Mike had hired the track for the day for some testing, but he let the Williams Formula One team use it to announce the return of Alain Prost and, man, there were some people there. It was almost like a race meeting, and they were just there to see him drive the car. Olivier Panis had set a lap time in a Formula 3000 at 13.5 on the circuit layout we were using on the previous day, so that was my little footnote for the day.

It was a bloody good field of drivers in Formula 3000 at the time, with guys who would make big names for themselves like Laurent Aiello, David Coulthard, Ruben Barrichello and Luca Badoer. In terms of my first benchmark, I was about half a second faster than Hideki, but I was two or three tenths of a second off the benchmark and still had plenty of things to fix to find that time.

I always had two rules for myself when testing a car in circumstances like these. First, don't stall when you first leave the pits, because you just look like a complete goose. Second, you've got to get out there and press on straight away. On the short circuit at Paul Ricard, there's a hard right turn just past the pit lane that hooks you onto the back straight. So, on that first lap I came blazing past the pits right into it. Mike apparently said to Fred, 'Jesus Christ, this kid's not mucking around.'

For me, that early impression was important. If you wanted them to be serious about you, you needed to let them know you were serious – and I was. We had terrible understeer in the slow corners, but in the quick ones – like Signes, the big right-hander off the back straight, which is an unbelievable corner and almost flat out – it was brilliant. But then you have a tight dipping right hander that reminded me of the Dunlop Loop at Amaroo, and the understeer was terrible there. We did two days of testing, but didn't get anywhere with the problem.

Then we headed off to Nogaro on the other side of France, and like Paul Ricard I'd never been there before. Jean-Marc Gounon had driven for 3001 International the previous year and Mike asked him to take me out and show me the track, so I jumped on the back of a moped and he gave me the inside running, which proved quite handy. It was a very different track to Paul Ricard. It had lots of slow corners I knew we would struggle with unless we found a cure for the balance issues.

It was a full grid of superstars and I went out on the track in the Reynard and was fastest straight away, and finished that session in seventh or eighth. Once I got out of the car, Mike took me out the back and I ran him through a lap in his Tarago. He was stunned; he said he'd never seen anything like it. He was rapt, and I thought I had a half a chance. But from there, I didn't go any faster and the others did. That understeer was killing us.

I learned after that weekend the really good cars at the top of the time sheets had a single-shock front set-up and we had twins. I was trying so hard, but it was just a dog on that track and I ended up crashing at Turn 1 and finishing a lap down.

The next week we went to Magny-Cours, now in the middle of France, and this was just the epitome of a modern Formula One track with fast corners and plenty of run-offs ... but it had no character, no bumps, no quirks to catch you out – just clinical. Even today's F1 drivers make the same comments and it rarely produces good racing.

On the plus side, it had fewer slow corners and it was faster, so that was going to be better for us. Malcolm Oastler was the chief designer at Reynard, and we were running a Reynard again so we sat down for a bit of a chat early in the weekend. He's Australian so we had rapport, and he ended up giving me a set-up sheet to make it go a bit better. The car was better, but still not good, and I ended up with only one racing lap.

What should have been a great time was a disaster – running a similar car to the Formula Holden but with 160 extra horsepower, which just amplified all the problems with the car. I was really cranky that in those two races we weren't able to show off what we could do.

It was a terrible experience for me. My back-up plan was always to spend the next year in Formula 3000, because I wasn't looking forward to racing a Holden back in Australia. But it was a lot of money we had to find and even though we had basically done a deal, we let it slide and I came home.

It was going to be hard to get the $1.5 million we needed; I mean, Australian companies have never been good at supporting our young drivers overseas and there was no television for the series either, so I shelved my international dreams and set my mind on dominating in Australia with a Holden.

Top left: Nissan Motorsport Europe test drive for Le Mans with the Group C sports car at Snetterton Circuit in England. This was thanks to Fred's great relationship with Howard Marsden, who was running the team.

Top right: Testing the Formula 3000 car with 3001 International team boss Mike Earle on the radio.

Middle left: Enjoying lunch with Thomas Erdos at Le Mans in 1997.

Bottom right: The start of Le Mans in 1997 driving the Lister Storm Jaguar with Julian Bailey and Thomas Erdos.

A NEW ERA   111

INTERNATIONAL MAN OF MYSTERY

In July 1993, between the final two races of the ATCC, I went over to France to run a Nissan in the French Touring Car Championship at Le Mans on the Bugatti circuit. It was so far from what we were doing in Australia at the time, but it was a lot of fun and a precursor to running in the Touring Car World Cup at Monza in October.

These cars were eventually what we referred to in Australia as two-litre touring cars. They were front-drive cars with four-cylinder engines and little attention paid to aero. They required a different driving technique; you really had to keep up momentum because they didn't have enough grunt to catch up and so lost ground easily. In contrast, our new Commodore racer had aero and plenty of grunt, just no tyres.

Alan Heaphy was running the team over there, and Nissan Australia funded my run there with Brad Leach putting the deal together. I think I finished seventh at Le Mans and then was nowhere at Monza, which was won by Paul Radisich who I'd eventually have some great dices with in Australia.

All the manufacturers were there for the World Cup and the driver line-up was awesome, but my equipment was just not good enough. Eric van de Poele and Kieth O'dor had the lightest spec engines available for the Nissan, while Ivan Capelli and I had the English engines. We were blown away by those two because Monza is just a drag strip.

I would get their data traces overlayed with mine – I had to get the scale right because the engineers running the team couldn't – and then I'd put them together and hold them up to the light. It was pretty clear Ivan and I were at a big disadvantage in a straight line. The Japanese heavyweights from Nissan who were there knew the cars weren't equal and they were happy with what we had achieved.

But it was a wild weekend. Julian Bailey passed me on his roof after a crash, which was pretty funny. Even with my lack of power I was going okay. But I went into the Parabolica and I was behind a couple of Alfas and a BMW and an Audi and they were just into it, and I went up the inside of them while looking for a top 10 finish. The Audi just turned in front of me like I wasn't there and that was it.

After the race I was talking with Mr Manabe, who was the highest-level Nissan guy at the track, and I was towing the party line of the day. But I told him that with the Japanese engine and the right engineering a young bloke – such as myself – could have won that cup in a Nissan. I took him and showed him what some of the others were doing, and explained that was what they needed to do if they wanted to win.

Some of those teams were so professional: they had the right numbers of engineers and spare parts and the like – they were fully committed. Nissan didn't do it to the same level and they never did win. That was my only outing in the World Cup.

At the 1993 World Touring Car Cup at Monza in Italy, where Tony Longhurst and I represented Australia.

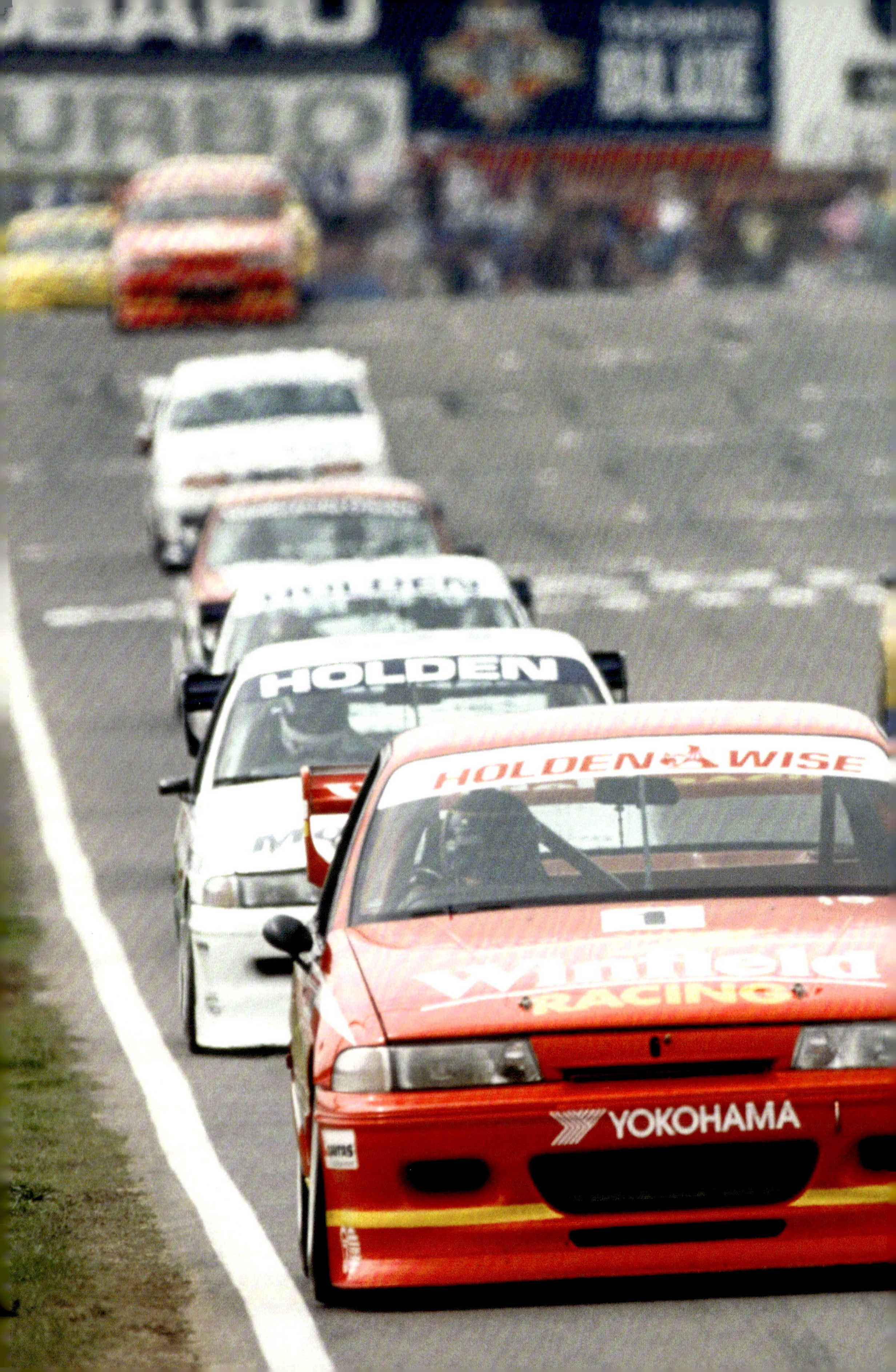
HOLDEN
HOLDEN WISE
Winfield
RACING
YOKOHAMA

With the Gibson Motorsport team, I made my first Bathurst 1000 start in a Holden in 1993 because changed rules meant Nissans were no longer eligible. Here I lead the pack in the early stages with only eventual winner Larry Perkins out of shot in front of the #1 Commodore.

Behind the wheel of my Winfield Racing Holden Commodore VP at Phillip Island in 1993.

THE HOLDEN SWITCH – AND SWEET REVENGE

We had farewelled the Group A cars at the end of 1992, which meant parting ways with the Nissan GT-Rs. We had to convert the business from a factory Nissan squad to whatever it would be for the 1993 season, which turned out to be a Holden. It was a big eye opener. Our first Commodore was just a customer car with bits and pieces from all over the place. As I said, we were looking after Bob Forbes's GIO GT-R, but he also had a Commodore and we started with that to test the Yokohama tyres.

We bought an engine from the Holden Race Team (HRT) that wouldn't fit when we tried to put it in the car. Something was a bit suspect there, I can tell you for a fact. We bought some stuff like front uprights from Ron Harrop and from Larry Perkins, but those were completely different too. Larry ran very little castor and it was set to only two degrees, while Harrop's was a cast upright with an offset bottom pin and six degrees of castor. We knew from that alone we had a lot to learn.

So when we arrived at the first race at Amaroo Park in 1993, the car was absolutely no better than any other customer car out there; anyone could buy the bits and put it together like we had. When I ran third at that meeting we were stoked. It was one of the greatest races of all time, by the way, and it will last with me forever. Glenn Seton and John Bowe beat me, but they'd been running these cars for a year, as had plenty who were behind me. We were also the first Holden to finish, and that was significant – to us, if no-one else.

By the time we got to Bathurst, we'd really started to get our program running. We had our own engines and were making the cars the way we wanted them to be. Bathurst was a great race – no Safety Cars and full speed all day – and we were a big chance to win when Jim had to go up the escape road at Murrays Corner to avoid a backmarker. We had the speed that day to win; we came from way back in the field to lead Larry in the closing laps, so that was gutting. It was easily the worst I had ever felt after a Bathurst up to that time. It would have been three in a row for us, and after the way we'd been treated on the podium the year before it would have been interesting. I ran a double stint to get us back into contention, and Richo said it was one of the best he ever saw at Bathurst, so that softened the blow a little.

Based on our performance and improvement we were looking forward to 1994 and we went out and brained them.

HOLDE
Skaife
Richards
TOOHEYS 1000
Winfield
RACING
YOKOHAMA

Hell Corner at Bathurst in 1993. Jim Richards and I narrowly missed out on winning our third straight Bathurst 1000, finishing just 10.5 seconds behind the similar Commodore of Larry Perkins and the late Gregg Hansford.

THE MOST SATISFYING TITLE: 1994

If you think about the scale of change that we'd gone through from the end of the GT-R program to getting into a Holden – starting competitively as a customer car and developing it into a full-on Gibson Motorsport car – it made 1994 very special. By the time we reached the end of 1993, we were in contention to win Bathurst, and we made a lot of progress with the car after that.

We went into 1994 with a real pep in our step because with all that work, including a very busy off season, we had our own car to race instead of some 'bitsa'. We'd basically made our own everything – front uprights, diff housings and the like – and we'd made solid progress on the engine with Gibsons' engine man Eric Schlifelner at the helm. We also had a completely new inlet manifold, which was done by a really clever guy called Murray Bunn, who was actually Jimmy Richards's mate from New Zealand.

We had a lot of serious development in the '93–'94 off season and when we wheeled the car out it was just fantastic. We improved the complete package and we were able to put it all to good effect in the first part of 1994. I won the first three rounds of the Championship and then was on the podium in the next five. The results of the final two rounds were a bit ordinary, but we'd already won the Championship and started looking to the next round of changes.

Given the criticism that we faced surrounding the GT-R's dominance – and everybody perceiving that we had a bigger tennis racket – I think for us to then move into a parity formula and line up against the Holden Racing Team and Perkins, and beat them, was significant and hopefully sent a message.

We weren't holding back on trying to get back to the pointy end again, and I personally just wanted to beat everyone. It was a very satisfying set of circumstances. It was a time for me that I look back on now and think, *Wow, that was bloody cool.*

As a driver, it was a time in my career when I felt like I was processing information really well and things were happening slowly in the car as a consequence. My decision-making was good and my raw speed was probably the benchmark in the category at the time. I consider this time, when I was 27, the first of two peaks in my career in terms of how I was driving.

RANDOM DRAW SETS UP ANOTHER WIN

You can see by the look on my face, when I drew the Number 1 in the Dash for Cash at Barbagallo in 1994 I knew I couldn't be beaten.

It was a crazy system, that: the top six qualifiers drew starting positions for a three-lap race, and the results of that race set the front three rows of the grid. Having secured the #1 for the Dash, I was going to start the main race from pole and I did all that and went on to win my second round of the season. By the time I won at Mallala three rounds later, I had sewn up the title with two rounds remaining, and that was an amazing feeling.

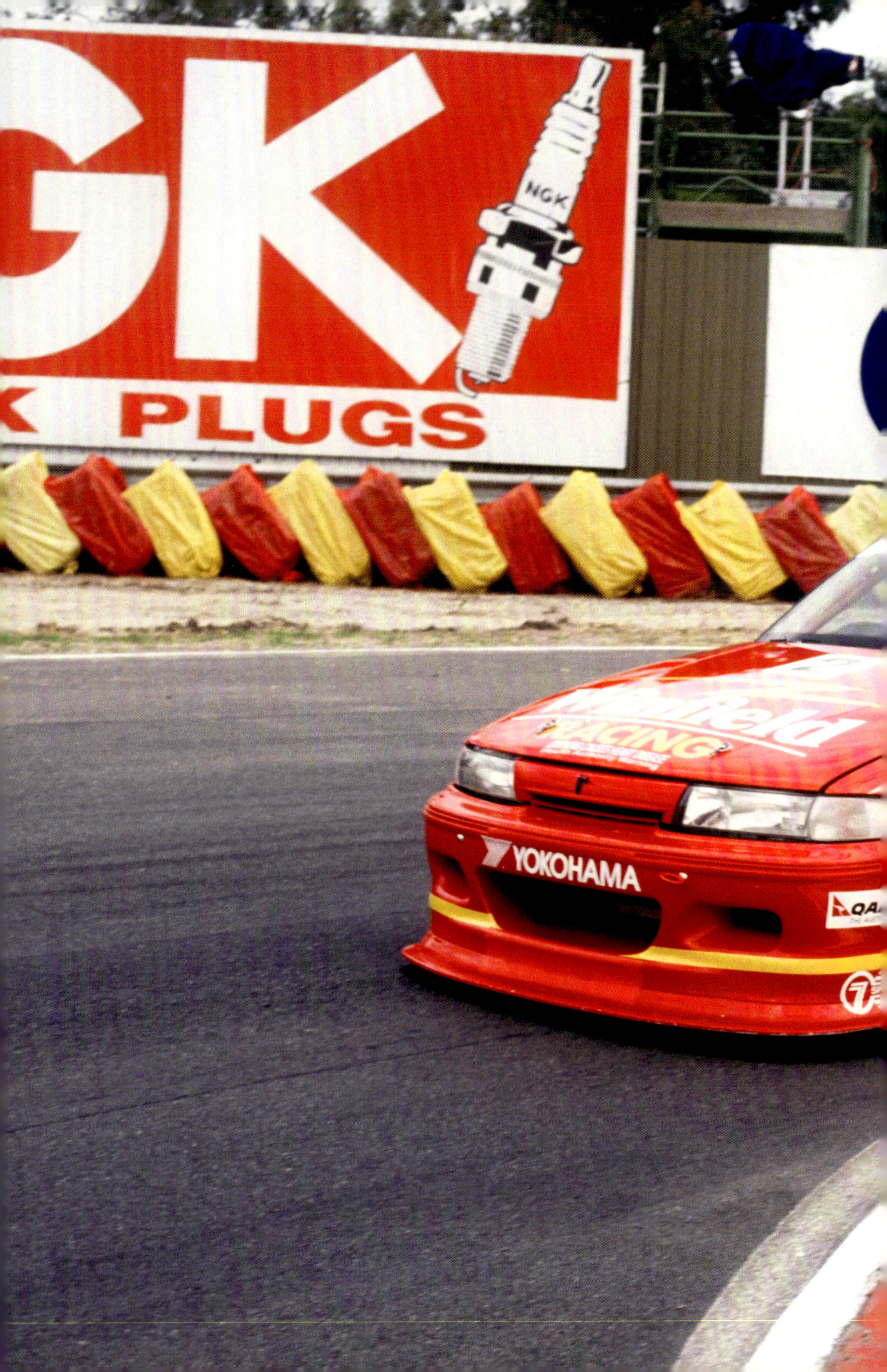
GK
K PLUGS
NGK
Winfield
RACING
YOKOHAMA

Sandown 1994: aboard my #2 Gibson Motorsport Commodore VP. Here I negotiate the corner onto the back straight at Sandown. I won both races to seal the overall round win, which gave me a solid start to the championship campaign. It led me to win Holden's first ATCC crown since Peter Brock in 1980.

MOMENTS THAT MAKE YOU QUESTION IT ALL

After winning that title in 1994, we followed up with an okay year in 1995, even though I started it on the bench, injured from a devastating testing crash at Eastern Creek. We had been doing wet weather tyre testing and I'd had the shits because they put the same tyres on the car instead of going back to a base tyre – it was the most ordinary tyre I've ever driven on.

I kept on saying, 'I don't even know why you're baselining it, just get it off the car and it'll never go back on again.' Anyway, I worked out the base line and I had the shits about it. I went barrelling down the straight thinking, *What a bunch of dickheads*. Driving this thing in these conditions with that tyre just wasn't fun.

At the end of the main straight, where the drag strip joins our track, there was drag compound on the road and that stuff is just like glass when it's wet. At one stage I turned the corner and the car just didn't look like making it and that's about the last thing I remember. It went off the road and hit the wall. I blacked out and woke up when they were dragging me out to the ambulance. The seat ended up in the back of the car and everything was broken; I was very lucky not to have been killed.

My first wife Belinda was pregnant with our son Mitch when that happened. She was in Melbourne and she came up to Sydney to Westmead Hospital where I was for a week or so. You'd have to be an idiot not to question what you did for a living at that stage. At the end of the day, it's what you do and the reality is that you make the decision to take those risks or not.

We know the sport's inherently risky and the mechanical failure thing is always the one that's scariest – when the brake pedal goes to the floor, or the throttle jams open, steering fails or a tyre blows. Those ones are all pretty wild because you have so little control, but the rest of the time you make an educated choice as to how much you want to put on the line.

As committed as you might be – and you might be right on the edge – you don't ever turn into a corner thinking, *I'm not going to make it*. But you have to set your own boundaries for how hard you want to push, how many risks you want to take, and I had a big think sitting in that hospital bed.

Heading the big pack of V8 Commodores and Falcons into the hairpin at Symmons Plains in Tasmania in 1995 – my first race after the big crash.

I had broken two vertebrae and dislocated some ribs. They call it a 'bucket-handle' dislocation, where the rib pops out at the back and at the front. I also had whiplash and all sorts of other stuff. I was pretty sore, and all the smartarses of the industry would come into the hospital and try to make me laugh because they knew it would hurt.

At the start of 1995 we had built a new car and we were organised, but then when I had that crash it put us behind schedule. So when I went out to Calder to drive the car after the crash I remember I was bloody nervous. I did four or five laps and it hurt like you wouldn't believe, although I had rib protectors on and all that stuff.

Even though I did the same lap time as Jimmy, and all the wiring seemed okay in my brain, there was no way I could race. So I missed the first round at Sandown a week later, which wasn't a good way to debut the #1 on the door. I qualified fastest in Tasmania for the next round though, and I knew then it was all going to be okay from there – although the season wasn't that great overall.

A test day crash at Eastern Creek in 1995. The paramedic is reaching in the door with Ivan Taylor, who was one of our lead mechanics, working to get me out of the car. Keith McCormack (Motorsport Manager, Yokohama) and Jim Richards are looking on with concern. I don't remember much of this dramatic aftermath.

NO SMOKE, NO FIRE

The crash aside, 1995 was tough for other reasons. The Federal Government was looking at legislation to ban tobacco sponsorship from the start of 1996 onwards. By the middle of the year we'd accepted this was coming and started looking around for new sponsors to replace Winfield. We had no small sponsors we could turn into big ones, so we had to start from scratch.

The previous year I had a clandestine meeting with John Crennan, who was running the HRT, and Tom Walkinshaw but I wasn't entertaining leaving Gibsons at that point in time. Then in 1995 they made me an offer. They spoke about what they were doing and what John's plan was with the business and how committed Tom was to that plan as well. At that time, HRT wasn't all that successful on the track and the two of them wanted to change that. A lot of John's plans relied on finding the right resources and building a business like Australian motorsport had never seen.

It was impressive and John's a very clever man, certainly one of the brightest motoring people I have ever met, but I had this real sense of loyalty to Fred and the team so I rejected them even though their offer was good. We had around 35 people at Gibsons, and many of them were and still are mates; I didn't want to abandon them.

I also knew if we had the money we could still do the job; I mean we could have easily won Bathurst that year again. We had speed and a fuel economy advantage when the tailshaft broke, and there was no way Larry was going to catch us otherwise. Who knows how different life would have been if we'd won that? Maybe we wouldn't have started 1996 in a plain white car?

I'd basically done a deal with Tooheys to come in as major sponsor with about half the money Winfield had been putting up, which was about $3.5 million at the time. When that fell over, we were on struggle street and we had to start putting people off. A lot of those guys went to HRT, which was interesting.

We got $1 million from Holden and also did a deal with Network Q for close enough to $400,000 for Bathurst, and that got us through to the end of the year. We had another deal with Sega, which was meant to be $400,000 but turned into $100,000 because the bloke ended up going broke.

Above: Tackling the short circuit at Eastern Creek in January 1996 in the opening round of the Australian Touring Car Championship. Gibson Motorsport ran a plain white Commodore, due to lack of corporate backing in the post-cigarette sponsorship era.

Left: Crossing the line to take seventh place in the 1996 AMP Bathurst 1000. We finished two laps down on the winning Holden Racing Team Commodore of Craig Lowndes and Greg Murphy – 12 months later I was part of the factory team myself.

All of that sent us into 1997 in a pretty lean state. I learned more about my sport in those first six months of 1997 than I had ever learned before. I was at the coalface, I was running around trying to do deals and then heading back to the shop to work on the car. But we were getting nowhere – I mean, we couldn't even do all the races.

Then Crenno called again and asked me to join Brock for the endurance races and then possibly replace him in 1998 since 1997 was his last season – well, theoretically, at any rate. It was not only a lifeline for me, but in the long run it was also good for Fred because John reached out and gave them a hand by getting them to run the Holden Young Lions, the manufacturer's racing-development program for emerging talent. Still, that first conversation with Fred was one of the hardest conversations I've ever had to have.

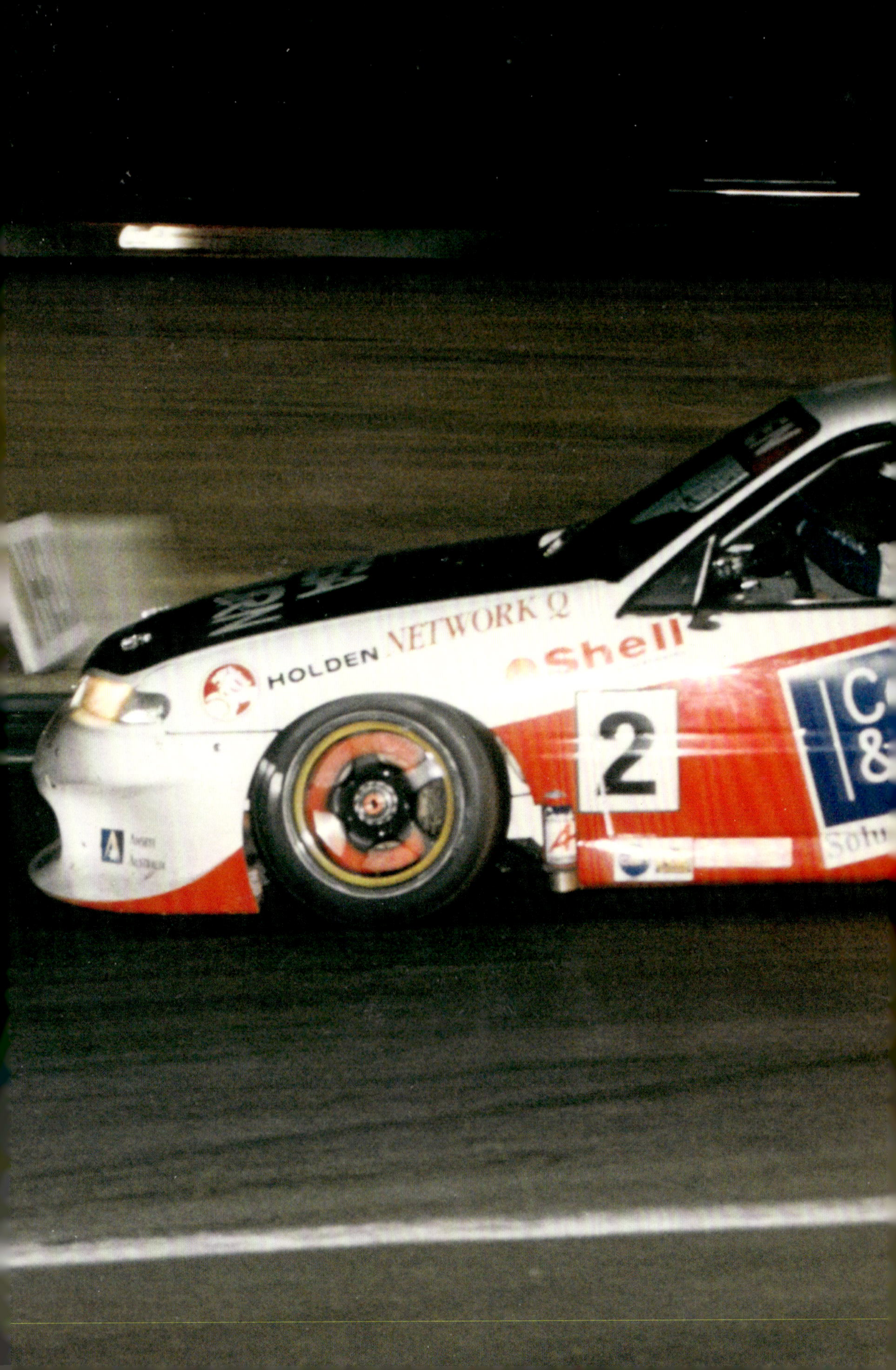
HOLDEN
NETWORK Q
Shell
2

The Commodore glows under brakes into the tight first corner at Calder Park in Melbourne in 1997. The first round of that year's Championship marked the beginning of the V8 Supercar era and was run under lights, hence the prominent glowing brake discs and exhaust flames.

MY VERY FIRST MOTORSPORT CHAUFFEUR
Words by Tony Cochrane, co-founder of V8 Supercars

MS, Skaifey and sometimes Mark, when we are debating a point, usually over a glass of personality (as he would say), is a first-class gem!

Quite rightly he is looked upon as one of the greatest race car drivers Australia has ever produced. His outstanding record of achievement demonstrates that in spades. He is a champion of the sport and is certainly up there with Brock, Moffatt, Johnson, Whincup and co. A colossus in every sense on the track and in my view a true champion behind the scenes as well – allow me to explain.

Much has been written and said about the spectacular growth and rise of V8 Supercars from the start of that era, replacing its predecessor, Group A touring cars. My fingerprints were all over it from day one; I wrote the original paper that concocted the entire concept, so I had a front row seat. It wasn't day one of my working up this idea that I first had the great pleasure of meeting MS, but it was pretty close to it.

As part of that process of trying to find out what made Australian motorsport tick and how it could be a bigger and more familiar sport to fans, both in Australia and overseas, I had various 'fact finding' meetings with some of the key players at the time: Perkins, Brock, Johnson, Cattach, Forbes et al. This led me on a cold Saturday morning in 1996 to the workshop of Fred Gibson on the outskirts of Melbourne, as I was very keen to hear his thoughts and ideas. Fred was his usual bright and engaging self. During this meeting he introduced me to his hot-shot young driver. They had had success but with the loss of cigarette money were facing a very challenging future. Indeed, that particular weekend a round of the Shell Series was taking place at Phillip Island and even though it was close by they did not have the budget to compete.

They say that when you meet someone who you really connect with you always remember the exact time/location of the meeting. The young hot-shot driver was Mark Skaife. Skaifey and I hit it off from the first introduction – he was a ball of energy and ideas, as competitive as anyone I have met (and I've met a good few). He was detail-focused, positive and had a massive desire to see Australian motorsport blossom and succeed. We were in an instant symbiotic relationship. It was to be the start of a great friendship that I still very much value nearly 25 years later. I didn't

With then AVESCO (Australian Vee Eight Supercar Company) Chairman Tony Cochrane in the drivers' parade at the inaugural Sensational Adelaide 500 in 1999. All three – Cochrane, me and the event itself – are members of the Supercars Hall of Fame.

know it that day, but he also had one outstanding quality I was to witness over a long period – his loyalty.

My original plan was to spend a couple of hours talking with Fred and then head to Phillip Island, which I stupidly believed was on the outskirts of Melbourne…? So after about an hour, MS said, 'Fred mentioned a taxi dropped you off – how are you getting to the Island?' Simple (so I thought) – 'I'll call another cab?' Well Fred and MS pissed themselves at my naivety. By then they both knew I wanted to go and visit a round of the Shell Series at a venue I had never visited before. MS was immediately on board – mate, I'll drive you down and show you around. It seemed like a stunning and simple plan. Let's go!

Of course, MS is a world-class talker – so I got chapter and verse on every detail of Australian motorsport. He left nothing out and he had me strapped in for 90-plus

A NEW ERA   133

minutes so he could belt my ears off – I was the captive audience. He never drew breath; both the car and I got a good workout! So, it's not a rumour, it's the absolute truth: Skaifey was my very first limo driver in motorsport! And boy did we get to go on one hell of a journey together over the next 16 years. We shared endless meetings, long drinking sessions, journeys all over the world, too many debates, lots of laughs and even some tears. I'd do it all again, if he would return as my chauffeur!

What started out as an unexpected discussion turned into a friendship and a business relationship, which helped take V8 Supercars to the very top. I was rapidly to discover that not only could this young gun steer like a competitive lunatic, but he was also just as gifted and just as keen to help evolve the business of touring cars. As he grew in the sport, so did his role on so many important committees and of course the Board of V8SA. We didn't always agree, but his goal was always to move us upwards and onwards as an exciting sport. As the Executive Chairman, it was my highly valued pleasure to have his talents on that Board.

As though that wasn't enough – the yabberer who could talk under water with a mouthful of ball bearings morphed into the media guy who worked tirelessly to ensure our TV pictures and output were first rate, as his racing years began to catch up with him. What a bloody package! That is why I credit him with so much that was great about that era. Yes, he was extraordinary behind the wheel of a Holden V8 Supercar, but he was also highly invested in how we set about changing, growing and developing the sport. He was the real deal in every sense, unlike some of the pretenders still around today.

Just in case you consider my view of Skaifey is all perfection, it is not. To prove we all have crosses to carry in life, he supports Collingwood! Now that is an issue; however, I'm pleased to say, our mateship has managed to survive this clear flaw in his (otherwise unblemished) character!

ock starting alongside Glenn Seton at the 1997 Bathurst from pole.

MARK SKAIFE WAS DIFFERENT
Words by John Crennan, former head of Holden Special Vehicles and HRT

My first encounter with Mark was in the Australian Airlines Flight Deck Lounge, Adelaide 1990. As I turned from the bar area with some adult beverages in hand for a few of our team members after a day at the track, the person behind me wearing a Nissan jacket said, 'Hi, Mr Crennan'. After my initial shock at receiving such a courteous greeting in the take-no-prisoners world of Motorsport, I then saw it was 23-year-old Mark Skaife and quickly insisted he call me John.

The 'Mr' bit threw me back to the 60s in GMH when, as junior members of staff, we would be candidates for getting the sack if we were to be so impertinent as to call any of the bosses by anything other than 'Mr'. After experiencing so much of that autocratic pompous nonsense in my early days at GMH, I was to become completely allergic to anyone calling me 'Mr'.

That's when my association with Mark started – 30 years ago. I have never forgotten Mark's formal greeting, as this was our first time we had any contact. This simple courtesy in 1990 typified why I saw Mark as so professional and 'different' from any other driver I'd known over my 25 years at HSV/ HRT and Kelly Racing.

Our race team leaders, like Jeff Grech, conducted the most important of all the selection criteria for recruiting a new factory driver, where the primary prerequisite would be the candidate's potential to win races and championships. My interest however, always centred on what incremental value the driver could add to our commercial and marketing operations and how they could assist in the growth of our business – everything from $20 T-shirts to $60,000 GTS cars.

My decision analysis for a new driver in the team always concentrated on certain questions. Will he be a good fit with the Holden heavies and the dealer organisation? Will he enhance relationships with our sponsor companies? Will he have the respect of the media? Will he be a role model sportsperson in the community? Will he be an outstanding ambassador for the HSV brand and be a key influencer with the enthusiast performance-car buyer? And will he be an advocate for teamwork and galvanise all members of the team with his commitment?

It was always a delicate task trying to mesh together the team's racing essentials and my off-track marketing wish list. However, we hit that jackpot when we signed

Mark to join our team in 1997. The complete package and ultimate professional in the race car, and a class act perfectionist who 'got it' when it came to our flow-on marketing and business plans.

Of the 14 mainstream drivers I ever penned a contract with, Mark was the only one I unilaterally decided to sign. I just did it, resolving to fight any battles or objections with other parties later. The rest is history as Mark delivered for the team in profound style on and off the track.

If I were to summarise in one word what the differentiator was with Mark, compared to the other big-name drivers in Holden's remarkable motorsport journey, it would be this: BUSINESS.

What separated Mark from his peers was his love and passion for developing and understanding business, as well as feeding his enormous appetite to grow his skills in management, leadership, marketing, product and brand, while still excelling behind the wheel. Equally, Mark would be constantly challenging himself to grasp every conceivable facet of the broader automotive industry – not just the motorsport segment.

Mark was astute and always planning ahead, with an ability to extend himself well beyond the 'sports bubble' so many other superstars can't see beyond. Mark's spectacular success makes me wonder whether the time has come when I should be addressing *him* as Mr Skaife!

HOLDEN
Mobil 1
PRIMUS TELECOM
VICTORIA BITTER
mycar
REVOLUTION RACEGEAR
Mark Skaife AB+

CHAPTER 6

THE FIERCE COMPETITOR
(THE HRT YEARS)

The Holden Racing Team (HRT) was a good team on the verge of greatness and I joined at the right time. They had started to win titles and Bathursts. When it was clear to me that Gibsons wasn't going to recover, I made the move to HRT. With the quality of the people there and the structures that were in place, I knew we could do something pretty special.

BUILD THE BEST TEAM, THEN PUT A FENCE AROUND IT

John Crennan is one of my best mates to this day, and he's a very clever automotive person. He doesn't try to be an engineer or anything like that, but his gut-feel marketing and sound business fundamentals allowed him to build the best racing team in the country … perhaps the best there had ever been to that stage.

How he rescued Holden Racing Team at the end of '95 – after one of the greatest disasters ever for a factory team at Bathurst – was just amazing. It was Houdini-like, how he got away with that one, and that was because he was ingrained in the GM system. He knew how the corporate thing worked and he outsmarted everybody. His work ethic, his intellect, his commitment to doing it really well and being able to create this tripartite thing in the GM world was first class.

When Bob Lutz, who ended up as a Vice Chairman of General Motors in the States, came out to Australia he basically acknowledged that this was the best example in the GM world of how to combine the mothership with special vehicles and a racing organisation: being Holden, Holden Special Vehicles and Holden Racing Team.

You don't get that sort of accolade unless the operation's pretty savvy, and in those days HRT was just a machine. Because I'd been running a lot of the business stuff at Gibsons, I had seen the way that John worked and some of his thinking when we sat down as team owners (TCI then TEGA), so moving from working with Fred, who I really admired, to John and Tom was an amazing step.

In 1996 HRT dominated touring car racing with Craig Lowndes winning the title, along with Bathurst and Sandown. But in 1997 Lowndes went to Europe and that left Peter Brock with a young and very quick Kiwi named Greg Murphy.

When the ATCC ended in 1997, I joined HRT and ran at Sandown and Bathurst as Peter Brock's co-driver. I qualified on pole at Sandown and that started a discussion around qualifying at Bathurst, but I did that as well and scored pole there too. I became the first driver to record a lap time under 2 minutes 10 seconds in the warm-up for the Shootout and then I won the Shootout by nearly eight-tenths of a second, so that was a pretty special day.

The 2 minutes and 9.89 seconds was completely unexpected. I only got one run in qualifying after Peter ran most of the session; he had clipped the wall trying to get a time and he'd bent the steering, and the best he could do was a 2 minutes 12.45 seconds, which we didn't think was going to be good enough to make it to the Shootout. I effectively got one run at it and did a 10.99 to qualify second behind Jason Bargwanna in the Holden Young Lions car, which was effectively a sister car to ours before Fred took over in 1998.

We had two runs in the Shootout warm-up the next day: the first was a 10.7 while roading tyres, which was the fastest lap for anyone that weekend, then on the second it was the 9.89 seconds, which was 1.3 up on the rest of the field. The car was a jet in race trim as well and we led that race from the start until it broke on Lap 52.

It was almost like I'd got in there and John had been able to demonstrate that things were going to be better than just okay. There was plenty of conjecture after Bathurst about who was going to replace Brock, and I had a very high level of confidence in John being able to deliver the right outcome for me. Brock had endorsed me as his replacement, but there were some in the team who wanted Murph, given Lowndes was returning. I eventually got the gig and the rest, as they say, is history.

Having Bob Lutz (Vice-Chairman of General Motors) at the 2002 HRT season launch was a pretty big thing at the time. Here you can see him as the second of the men in red shirts in the front row, with John Crennan on the aisle adjacent to him. Jason Bright and I are also in red shirts – that's us in the front.

THE FIERCE COMPETITOR   141

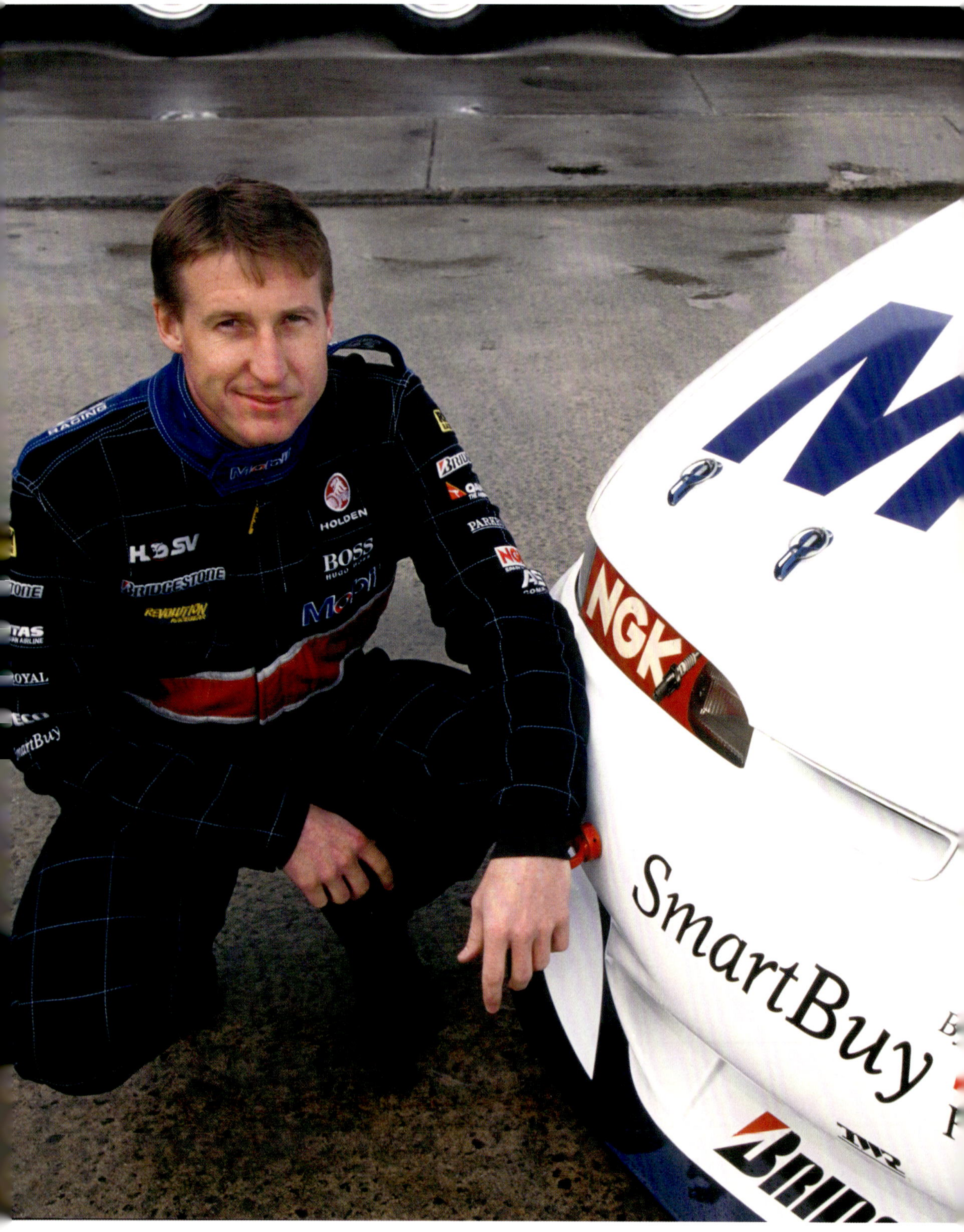
HOLDEN
BOSS
BRIDGESTONE
NGK
SmartBuy

In many ways it was an honour to drive with Brock in his famous #05 car, but I also had my eye on the bigger picture for 1998 with Brock's planned retirement after Bathurst in 1997.

THE FIERCE COMPETITOR **143**

144 MARK SKAIFE

Aboard the famous #05 Mobil Holden Racing Team Commodore I shared with Peter Brock at Bathurst in 1997. I put the car on pole after a sizzling lap time in the Top 10 Shootout. My debut with the Holden Racing Team in 1997 brought instant success – I put the famous #05 Commodore on pole position for the Sandown 500 in Melbourne.

Sharing a quiet moment behind the scenes with PB at Bathurst 1997.

146　MARK SKAIFE

TWO BROCKS

By 1997, I'd learned that there were manifestly two Peter Brocks, in that he had forged a career as a racing car driver (Brock 1) and got to a point where he had the biggest and best brand in the sport (Brock 2). After the debacle of 1987 when he got dumped by Holden, he somehow found a way to come back in and be a factory driver for the marque again. If you talk about John's Houdini act in 1995, Brock's was even bigger, but such was his popularity that he could fix something people thought could never be mended.

I knew Brock fairly well, but obviously had never been inside his camp. He was a beautiful and natural driver and was great with people – and that was it. He knew the power of the people. He'd get out of the car during those two races I did with him and didn't say anything about the car – he just walked straight to the back of garage to sign autographs. I remember thinking to myself, *How did he ever get a good car to race?* I'm sure back in the '70s and '80s he was much more like how I was then, but he'd worked out that his ticket to ride in 1997 was his popularity and he was looking after that. I just worked on the car with the team to see what we could do.

But give him a car, tell him it's good, and he'd race like it was, regardless of its state. In that Bathurst he had a great battle early on with Larry Perkins and broke the lap record, and when Craig Lowndes crashed behind me during my stint we could have just put our arm on the window and cruised to a win ... until the car broke of course.

I got on really well with Peter – not one ounce of drama and I think there was a healthy respect both ways. I took my role effectively as his replacement very seriously.

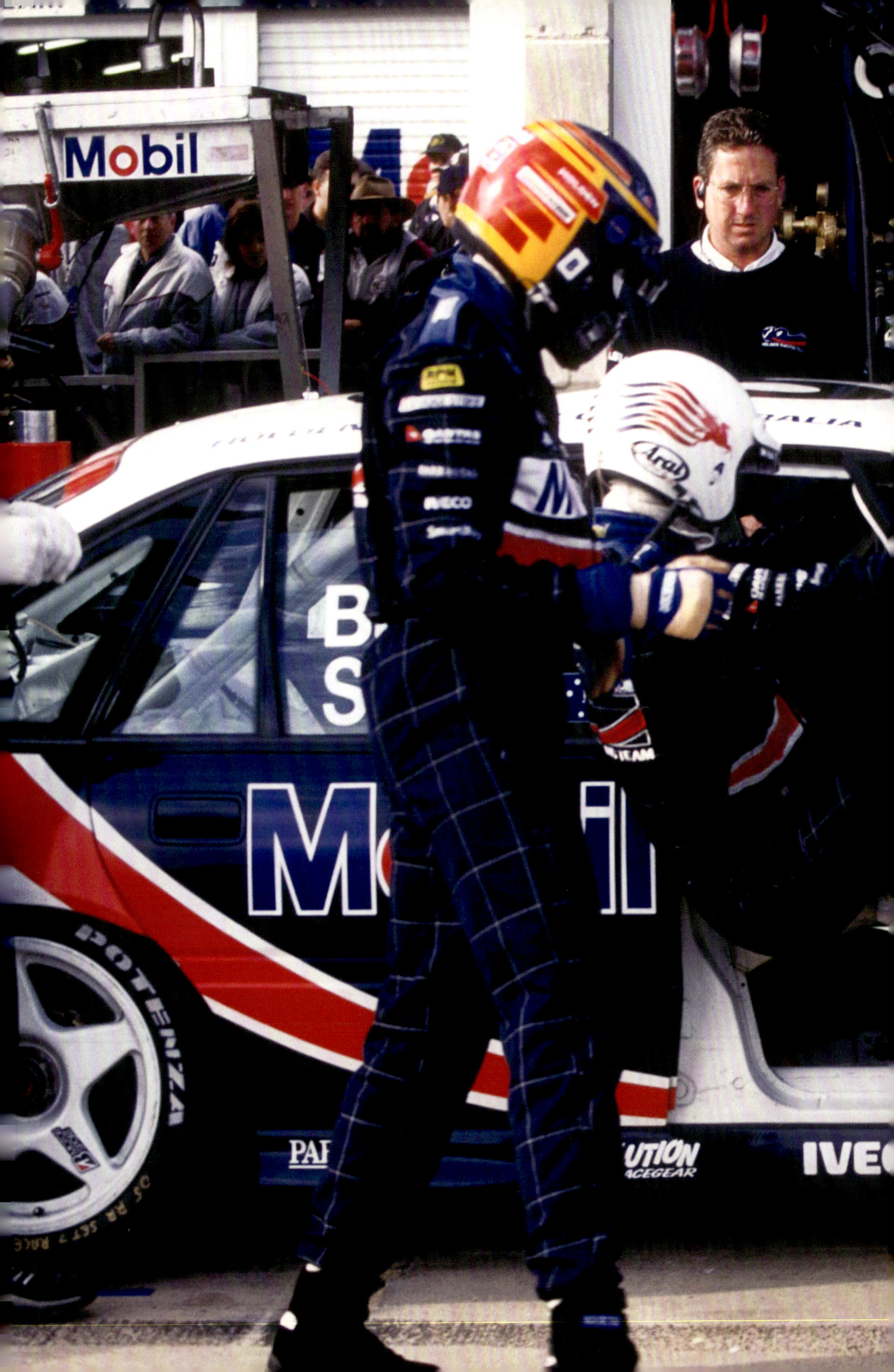
Mobil
Mobil
IVECO
POTENZA
Arai

Peter Brock steps out of the #05 Mobil Holden Racing Team Commodore VS at Bathurst in 1997 with me behind him. Standing behind me is Alex Marchese. Looking on from the other side is Tony Fredriksson, and Ron Harrop (with the headphones on) is timing our driver practice change.

THE FRIEND AND FAMILY MAN
Words by David White, former Head of Sport at Network Ten

In April 1997, I had been appointed to the position of General Manager of News, Current Affairs and Sport at Network Ten. Based in Sydney, I was very attracted to the role for the opportunity it gave me to shape the sports portfolio of the Network. I had a lifelong interest in motorsport and was committed to the development of the newly formed V8 Supercar category, as it was known then.

Six weeks later, I had a meeting with James Erskine from IMG. James was a board member of AVESCO – the controlling body of the category – and he told me that Mark Skaife did not have the budget to compete in the series, and that as a two-time champion and hero of the sport, he was very important to the appeal and success of the category. He asked for $50,000 from Network Ten and I agreed on the single condition that I needed to meet Mark first. After all, I thought it reasonable to at least make my own decision as to whether Mark was a dickhead or not – in which case the $50k would go to a much better home!

We met in Studio 4, a trendy new café in the same complex as the Network Ten offices. He arrived on time, immaculately and fashionably dressed, greeted me with a firm handshake and a professional smile and to my great surprise showed not one trait of being a dickhead. He was grateful for my time and spoke enthusiastically about how he planned to make his mark in the series and with Holden. Little did I know then just how successful he would go on to be, both on and off the racetrack. The money was his.

Mark didn't win much that year but he certainly won my friendship. We rapidly moved on from coffee and cake to Borolo and fine fare. In fact, I would love to know how many great restaurants we have enjoyed each other's company in.

It was during one such meal a few years later that he asked me who the attractive Production Manager was that I had assigned to managing the Outside Broadcast logistics at each of the V8 race weekends. Toni Strachan was a highly qualified, intelligent, ambitious woman who had not the slightest interest in becoming a car racing driver's object of affection. I told Mark exactly that. However, it did not come as a huge surprise to receive a call from Mark one evening, when he told me that he and Toni were enjoying strawberries and champagne at a fashionable Sydney roof top bar!

Mark and Toni have of course been married for many years now and have two beautiful daughters – Mia-Rose and Tilly – the latter being my adorable god daughter.

I have lived with my family in London and New York since 2014 so the frequency of our lunches and dinners with Mark and his family have been curtailed. However, when we do meet a couple of times each year, I am pleased to say that our friendship is as strong and rewarding as ever and that the restaurant bills never get any smaller.

David White (left) and Craig Kelly (right) with Mitch and me at my wedding to Toni.

Toni and I first met when she was production manager at Network Ten Sport, working for David White. We married seven years later at Raes on Wategos, Byron Bay, in August 2004. Hugo Boss made a special suit from the same material as the groomsmen's for Mitch, complete with matching tie.

Toni in the driver's seat and with me at Bathurst.

THE FIERCE COMPETITOR 153

Phillip Island, 1999.

FINDING MY FEET WITH HRT

For me 1998 was a pretty interesting year because I qualified really well, but I wasn't getting the race wins. I made a few silly mistakes, like thinking John Bowe would yield a corner he had clearly lost. He didn't.

But I did learn something from Crenno that day. This was the first race of the season, and he came up to me afterwards and told me that what he'd seen wasn't great risk management, which I didn't understand. I was there to race and win every time I went out, but the system at the time was that you started the second race where you finished the first, which meant it paid to be cautious in that first race. In John's eyes, taking a risk in the first race wasn't worth it; all I needed to do was finish second and then beat him in the next race, instead of starting down the order and having no chance. It started to change the way I thought about some races and I started playing the numbers game a little more. If I didn't understand the importance of playing the numbers in 1998, 1999 certainly cemented it for me.

Over time I've been pretty lucky with whoever has been on the race radio with me, and they have played a big role in walking through the numbers games with me. If the car wasn't good enough, they had to talk me into accepting that and getting the best result we could on the given day. Maybe we could have won in 1999 if we'd been better in the two double-points races, for instance. They were my two worst rounds for the year and I gave away 468 points to Craig, which was way more than he beat me in the series by. I won six rounds of the 13-round series and Craig only won two, but he still beat me. I needed to be smarter.

I'd started to understand the differences in terms of what you needed from a qualifying car and a race car on Bridgestone tyres, and that was helping. In 1998 I got pole at Bathurst with a record lap, and then in 1999 I just missed to Mark Larkham who did a ripper lap. I was quicker than Craig but not putting together each weekend as well, so he was beating me in the series.

Rob Starr was brilliant with me at the time; he really understood how to read my feedback and then prioritise changes, or talk me down from the ledge, so to speak. He came over to my car in 2000 and we built a great rapport quickly, and you saw that with the results. I was also much more consistent and better at maximising my returns week-in, week-out.

LOWNDES AND SKAIFE: CHALK AND CHEESE
Words by Craig Lowndes, racing driver and former teammate

Personality-wise, Mark and I are chalk and cheese. But I think that actually worked in our favour when he joined HRT, and again later in life when we reunited to race with Triple Eight.

When he first joined HRT there was a little angst on the workshop floor; we had a lot of ex-Gibson workers there and they weren't that keen on him coming in, but it proved to be nothing and he just fitted in. But Mark was quickly into every nut and bolt with his attention to detail. I remember him being in the engine shop, wanting to know what map, what cylinder head … he was into every facet of a race team, and I was the complete opposite.

I remember walking onto an aeroplane once and Mark was sitting there with an engineering book and studying up on geometry and suspension and aerodynamics. He was always pushing to understand every element of a car. My whole career, all I've really focused on is the driving part of it.

I've always respected Mark as a driver; we just operated differently. He'd even spend twice as long, if not longer, getting the seat position right, the seatbelts right, the steering column. Everything had to be perfect for him.

We got to drive at Bathurst together with HRT in 1998 and 2000 because the rules allowed you to pair your top drivers back then. So, like everyone else with two cars, we threw our eggs in the same basket. Physically we are a similar height, but he's got really long legs and a short torso. So when we actually drove together in the car, I was struggling because the steering wheel was too close to me. And then, of course, vice versa for him: where I wanted the steering wheel was too far away. So the team came up with a two stage column, so when we did a driver change we could push the steering wheel away for me and then bring it closer for him.

I think we had a healthy rivalry inside the team. He wanted to beat me and I wanted to beat him, but we weren't doing anything that would hurt the team. I never tried to stitch him up over anything, and I don't think he ever tried to on me. It was just leaning on both of our strengths, and his was detail and analysis. Most people think of four stages for a corner – braking, turn in, middle and exit – but Mark had it in about 15 stages, almost like metre by metre. He was super critical about what he wanted from a car.

At a race weekend he was focused. He hated me going out and signing autographs – to the point that he asked me to stop. 'No. For god's sake don't sign anything because it makes me look bad.' He was focused on the data and our brains worked differently. Away from the track I think he relaxed, he opened up more. He really enjoyed catching up with mates and having a drink and just really being normal.

When I switched to Ford after the 2000 season, I got the full set of Skaife mind games. He was always in the media saying it wasn't the Ford that was hopeless – it was the team and the drivers not doing a good enough job. It didn't bother me. Juan Pablo Montoya was my teammate when I did Formula 3000 in Europe, and he was the master of mind games – he would mentally just kill you – so after that I could cope with anything from Mark. But I saw what it did to others. He was a master.

Left: 1998 Indy on the Gold Coast.

Below: 1999 Adelaide 500.

158   MARK SKAIFE

HE WAS ALWAYS GOING TO MAKE IT
Words by Glenn Seton, racing driver and childhood friend

Over time Mark and I ended up having some great battles on the track. There was one race at Phillip Island in 1999 or 2000 where we had ding dong battle from start to finish. He ended up beating me that day and it was on. He was a hard and fair racer, and that day either of us could have punted the other many times, but we never had any meaningful contact and that was what made it so memorable. Eventually we did recover our friendship after our brief fallout, but it made no difference. On the track we were rivals and we needed to beat each other.

Mark was always going to make it. He was always very determined and very well educated in a motor racing sense. He had an eye for engineering and detail, which was very important back in those days.

I look at a few things when rating a race driver and he ticked all the boxes and then more. He had ambition, he had hunger, he had determination and he had very good technical and driving skills to back it up. He was also a thinker; he planned his moves and he worked on race strategy with his team, and he had a lot of motor racing intelligence and education. When you put all those things together you end up with a pretty impressive package, and I put him right up there with the Geoghegans, the Moffats, the Brocks, all those guys. You don't achieve what he's achieved by not being pretty good at what you do.

At the end of the day we have a friendship that was founded at motorsport, but there is much more than just motorsport. We had some great times away from the track, and I always felt that he would back me if we ever got into trouble, which was important, although more likely it was him who was getting into trouble.

Some people don't like Mark and see him as pretty opinionated. But to win in motor racing you have to be single-minded, you've got to be quite hard and forceful to get what you need to do the job. He did all of that and he was winning races and championships for two decades as a result.

THE OBSESSIVE OVER-ACHIEVER
Words by Richard Hollway, former HRT lead engineer

To sum up Mark in one sentence, I would describe him as a total professional who was 100% focused on winning, but off the track he loves a beer and is a lot of fun to be around.

I first met Mark when he came to drive for the Holden Racing Team (HRT) in 1997 as Peter Brock's co-driver for his final endurance races ... no pressure – if he stuffed it up, half of Australia would blame him for ruining the Australian motor racing icon's grand finale. Yet he did an outstanding job, putting the car on pole with the first 2:09 min ever around Bathurst. My favourite photo of all time is of this lap, with him coming into the grate with three wheels in the air!

He returned in 1998, entering a team that was very much focused around Craig Lowndes – rightly so as Craig had won the Championship in 1996, went to Europe in 1997 and returned as the HRT golden boy in 1998. Half of the team were ex-Gibson Motorsport, where Mark was both a driver and General Manager, so there was an element of hostility towards him.

In a factory race team, each car effectively competes with the other car – the first rule is to beat your teammate. Mark worked hard on developing a core group of people around him who all knew he was dedicated, tenacious and would give his utmost always. And this pushed us to do the same.

Over the years at HRT working with Mark, I learned more about race engineering than from any other driver. You could never question his commitment or effort when it came to doing what he loved, and he was the most organised bloke I ever met; some would call it OCD ...

He used the data like no driver I had ever worked with, and his ability to simplify the behaviour of the car for us to understand how he wanted the set-up was a huge advantage. He would write scribbly notes to describe the chassis from initial turn-in to clearing the brake to picking up the throttle, which added massive value to the engineering team. In the end, if you gave him what he wanted, he only went faster.

Mark is a driver who genuinely and absolutely LOVED the game – the engineering, the battles, the sports psychology. I don't recall working with any other driver who just loved driving fast and on the limit so much. Mark has a Steve Smith-like obsession with driving.

His real personality is a total contrast to his professional and polished corporate and TV image. Off track and away from the game he is a ratbag who takes the piss out of everyone and has a seriously warped sense of humour. His favourite stories always seem to involve someone being hurt or 'maimed'. I'm not sure if this is a Skaife trait or a New South Wales Central Coast thing – either way it's fun to be around.

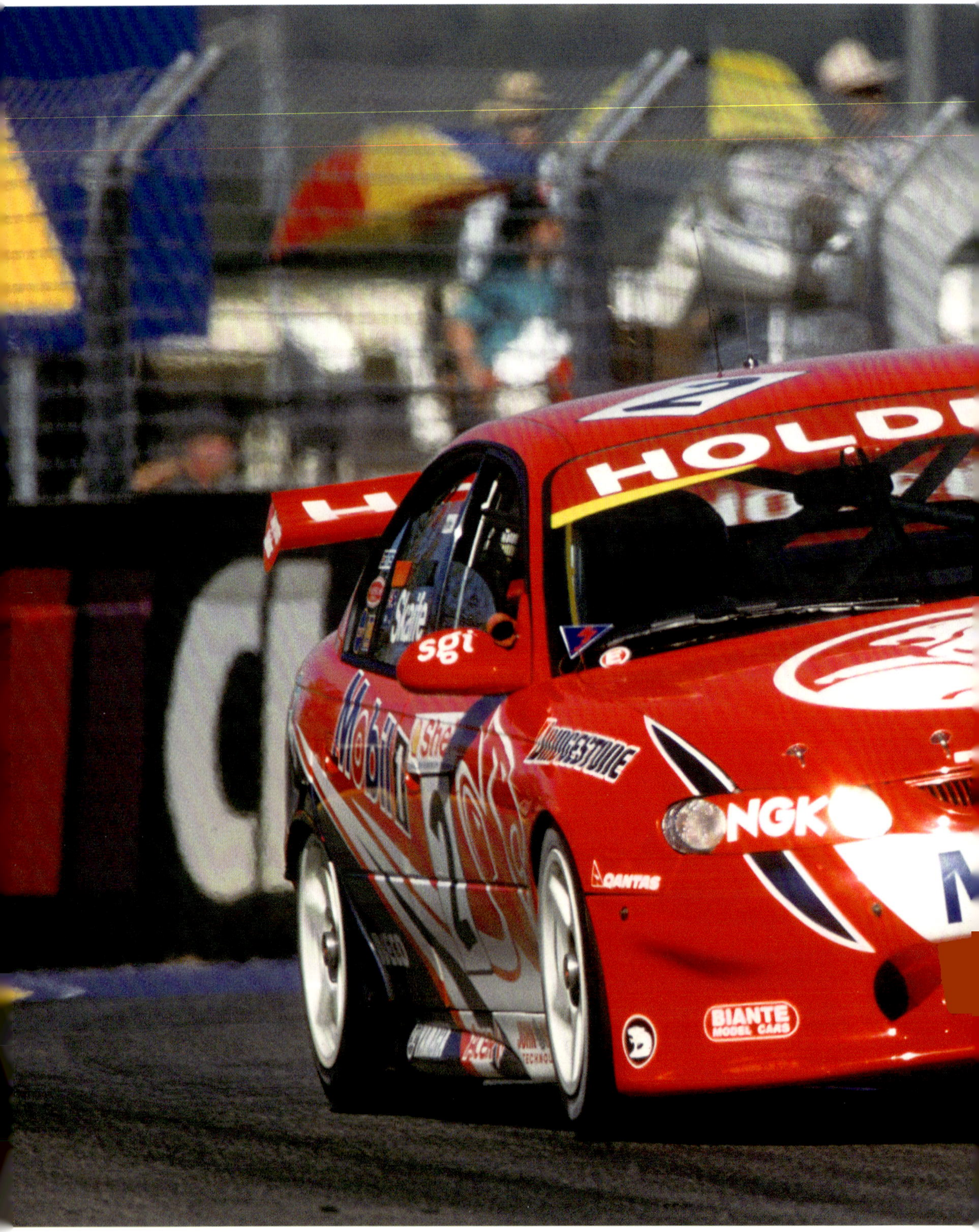
sgi
NGK
QANTAS
BIANTE
MODEL CARS

Bouncing off the kerbs through the Senna Chicane at the 2000 Clipsal 500 in Adelaide.

Entering the pits at Phillip Island in 2000.

On the track (left), holding off Jason Bargwanna and Garth Tander at Adelaide in 2000, and on the podium (right). I started last in the 38-car field and, despite a pit lane penalty, still managed to win the race. It was one of my greatest victories.

THE THREE-PEAT

Each year in motorsport, there is always someone who jumps up and makes a statement. In 2000 that was Garth Tander, but even though he finished second in the Championship and won Bathurst, it didn't diminish the intensity or the importance of my battle with Lowndes. Lowndes had won three titles in HRT cars, and all the talk for most of the year was that he was going to leave the team and even go to Ford, which was eventually all confirmed.

In my mind, I wanted to beat him at HRT. I wanted those two years of learning to count for something. So it was satisfying to beat him and to win with him at the Queensland 500, since we were paired together for the endurance races. I was solid and consistent early in the Championship and that set me up to win, so long as Bathurst wasn't a disaster.

Bathurst was the last race of the season that year and I had a good lead over Tander heading into that race. If he won Bathurst I only had to finish 17th to win the title, but I just wanted to win the race and send Craig off on a high in his last ride for HRT. It was going well and the real battle for the lead on lap 114 was between Neil Crompton, Tander and me.

Matt Neal was a lap down but he decided to race us, and went up the inside of Crompo and hit him. I still laugh when I think of what Crompo said later: 'I'd never been dive-bombed by a wobbling backmarker before.' He was driving with Glenn Seton that day, and they absolutely had enough speed to win, and this joker took him out. I hit the back of him because I had nowhere to go, and that was close to ruining my day. The steering was bent and two laps later I got a flat tyre, which I had to get fixed.

When I got back on the track I asked Rob where I was and he said 17th. 'And where is Tander?' He was leading, so we set off. I couldn't drop a spot or I'd lose the Championship, but we got into it and I finished sixth. It was a frustrating race because we probably should have won; the car was absolutely excellent. Craig did a really good job too and it would have been a nice send off for him. But it wasn't to be.

Even on the Sunday night at Bathurst, Tom was still trying to get Craig to stay. I knew that John was far from happy with Craig and the people advising him.

Above: I was crowned Shell Championship Series Champion in 2000, collecting the V8 Supercar Champion's gold wreath after that year's Bathurst 1000.

Left: A moment to celebrate victory in the opening round of the 2001 Shell Championship Series for V8 Supercars at Phillip Island.

Tony Longhurst and I heading for the win in the 2001 Bathurst 1000.

WWW.V8SUPERCAR1000.COM

Celebrating victory with Tony Longhurst at Bathurst in 2001. I'd won twice before in a Nissan – in 1991 and 1992 – while Tony had won the 1988 race in a Ford Sierra. This was my first win at Bathurst in a Holden.

Tony Longhurst and I won the 2001 Bathurst 1000 in this #1 Holden Racing Team Commodore VX.

John also had a management contract with Craig that he was breaking, but this was big and it was pretty clear Craig was moving on. This was the only time someone went from Factory Holden team to Factory Ford team, other than when Colin Bond went across to Moffat's team in 1977. The funny thing is Craig joined a new Ford team being set up by Fred Gibson!

We had some great battles over the next two years. Fred had certainly proven again that when he had the finance in place he could build a great team. Craig was a bit inconsistent in 2001 but I dominated, with nine wins from the 30 races and 20 podium finishes to win back-to-back titles – this time from Russell Ingall, with my new teammate Jason Bright in third. A Bathurst win with Tony Longhurst capped off the 2001 season.

Then we went back and did even better in 2002 to beat Greg Murphy – who was running in a second team that we were essentially running, which didn't make me happy – and Marcos Ambrose who was emerging for Ford. I won more than half the races that year and won the first five rounds before getting beaten by Brighty. I should have won that too but Bondy gave me a shit penalty and I was feral – before winning again next start. That was six wins from the first seven rounds and the title was virtually over.

It's funny though – between 2001 and 2002 the only thing we changed on the car was that the red on the back of the car became a red, black and white chequered flag. I couldn't believe it; nothing else changed, even though we went from Bridgestone to Dunlop tyres.

I decided to use the fact that we had the four cars and ran pre-qualifying for the Clipsal 500 instead of Rick Kelly. That was one of the great days in motorsport. Those last five minutes of the final session at Mallala were dead-set out of control and I had to do one of the best laps I've ever done just to get to the 'real' race meeting. The reason I wanted to do that session was to get some extra laps early on the Dunlop tyre. As it turns out the new tyres suited our car perfectly, which is why we started the season so well.

Not everyone was happy with us during that period; we earned all sorts of tags, like the 'Evil Empire'. But John had built the best team and he did build a big fence around it ... only he started to expand the size of that fence with a second and then a third team as well. This move was building barriers across the

Leaping across the kerbs at Sandown in the final round of the V8 Supercar Championship Series in 2002. I was crowned the champion for the third year in a row.

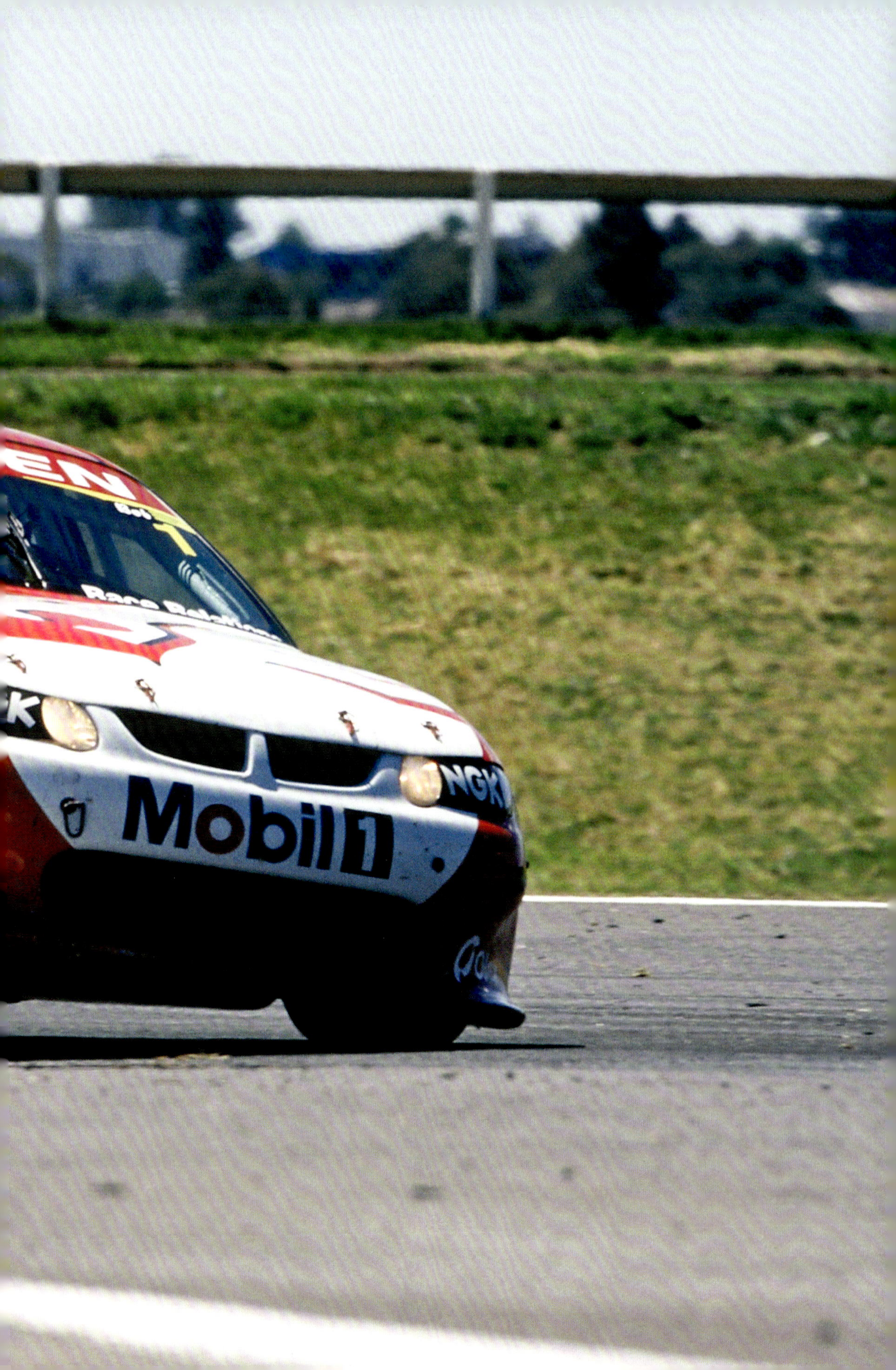

Mobil 1
NGK

Bathurst, 2002.

Above: Flames spit from my HRT Commodore at Sandown in 2002. This is the car we dubbed the Golden Child because it helped us to two championships, two Bathursts and two Clipsal wins.

Left: I was officially crowned V8 Supercar Champion for the third straight year after the final round of 2002 at Sandown. I shared the podium with Marcos Ambrose, left, and Greg Murphy, right. Ambrose won the next two championships in 2003 and 2004.

THE FIERCE COMPETITOR 175

board: the media didn't like us much, the Ford teams cried parity and the other Holden teams just wanted to know what we were doing.

We weren't that fussed how they felt; we were just doing our job. But we also had good fan support. I don't think you could count the number of the HRT jackets that were sold in a season – it was a staggering number. But it was what it was. We were the best team in the country, and we were going to protect and defend that at any cost.

I think Bathurst 2002 was my best win ever, and it was made all the better by doing it with Jim again – 10 years after our last win there together. It must have been hard for Jim's wife, Fay, though, because we had to beat his son Steven to win the race in what was a great battle from the start to the end. Jim had no qualms; he was there to win and he didn't care if it was his son he beat or not.

It was funny on the podium – Jim took the microphone and played up the 1992 podium by greeting the cheering crowd with, 'You're a pack of very nice people,' which was funny. This was the second peak of my career. Obviously winning the third title in a row, my fifth overall, was great, but winning Bathurst with Jim again was just the cream on top.

THE MOST SPECIAL BATHURST WIN
Words by Jim Richards, Kiwi racing driver and former teammate

In 2002 Mark rang me and asked what I was doing for Bathurst, to which I replied 'probably not a lot'. So, he asked me to come and drive for HRT. There was no guarantee I was going to drive with him; in fact in the lead-up race in Queensland I drove the second car with Tomas Mezera.

But I did drive with Mark at Bathurst and we won, 10 years after our previous win there and our third one together. I was 56 or something and definitely a co-driver. I just didn't want to do anything wrong to upset his Championship, so I was very careful and I didn't feel I drove that well. I knew I wasn't going to win another one, which makes 2002 special, and to do it with Mark was just fantastic.

We had some great times together and he was fun to drive with, but so competitive. There was a time at Lakeside when he asked, 'How are you going under the bridge? Are you going flat?' I said, 'Yeah, no problem,' even though I wasn't. So he said that next time out he'd give it a go because that was where he thought he was losing most of his time. I said, 'Don't do it on the first or second lap because I'm not going out in the next session and I would love to go up to that corner to watch – I haven't seen a big accident for a while!' We used to tease each other like that, but it was great fun… of course you'd never let him do something stupid without letting him know first, but he was always up for a challenge.

Mark, to me, was just a really good kid, a great lover of cars, generous to a fault and we got on really, really well. We don't see each other as much these days because I am flat out doing nothing and he is flat out doing everything, but he's still a great mate and there is such a strong bond there.

THE FIERCE COMPETITOR

THE PERFECT STORM

I'm not going to go into too much detail here about what went on with Tom Walkinshaw at the end of 2002. Suffice to say he had a few legal and solvency issues, primarily out of the Formula One stuff with Arrows, which had a massive impact on the Holden Racing Team.

Tom had to offload his shareholding and it went into the temporary care of Holden before I bought it. Unfortunately for me, Holden decided to sell only the race team and not the full operation, and that left me trying to do it all with one hand tied behind my back, forced to use Holden Motorsport as my main supplier. John Kelly and Kees Weel had bought the other two teams, and they were both independently wealthy, but for me this was my whole life and I needed to make it work. I had loan repayments to meet, after all.

As anyone reading this book would probably know, it eventually imploded and I was left with the choice of trying to buy Tom out of Holden Motorsport (after he had taken control of that from Holden), or selling HRT back to him. The latter is what I decided to do at the end of 2008, after five years of running the team. I certainly came across a lot of snakes in that period, and interestingly none of them have anything to do with top-level motorsport anymore so that tells a story. I also think most people are aware of the true story and that I don't need to defend myself against the lies and rumours of the day.

But for us heading into 2003, it was all about the timing of those issues and the arrival of Project Blueprint, and together they made a perfect storm for us. Blueprint was the biggest set of engineering changes for the Holden teams in more than two decades. You couldn't believe the amount of work and effort we had to put in just to remain competitive. All the guys like Crusty (Richard Hollway) and Robbie Starr set about trying to get the transition working, and they did an amazing job really.

We came out and won the first round at Adelaide in 2003, which was just unbelievable considering everything that was going on. In many ways it was just great to be sitting in the car and escaping the shitfight.

With co-driver Todd Kelly celebrating victory in a wet Sandown 500 in Melbourne in 2003. The win was my second Sandown 500 win and came 14 years after my first in 1989.

THE FIERCE COMPETITOR 179

On the grid at 2001 Clipsal.

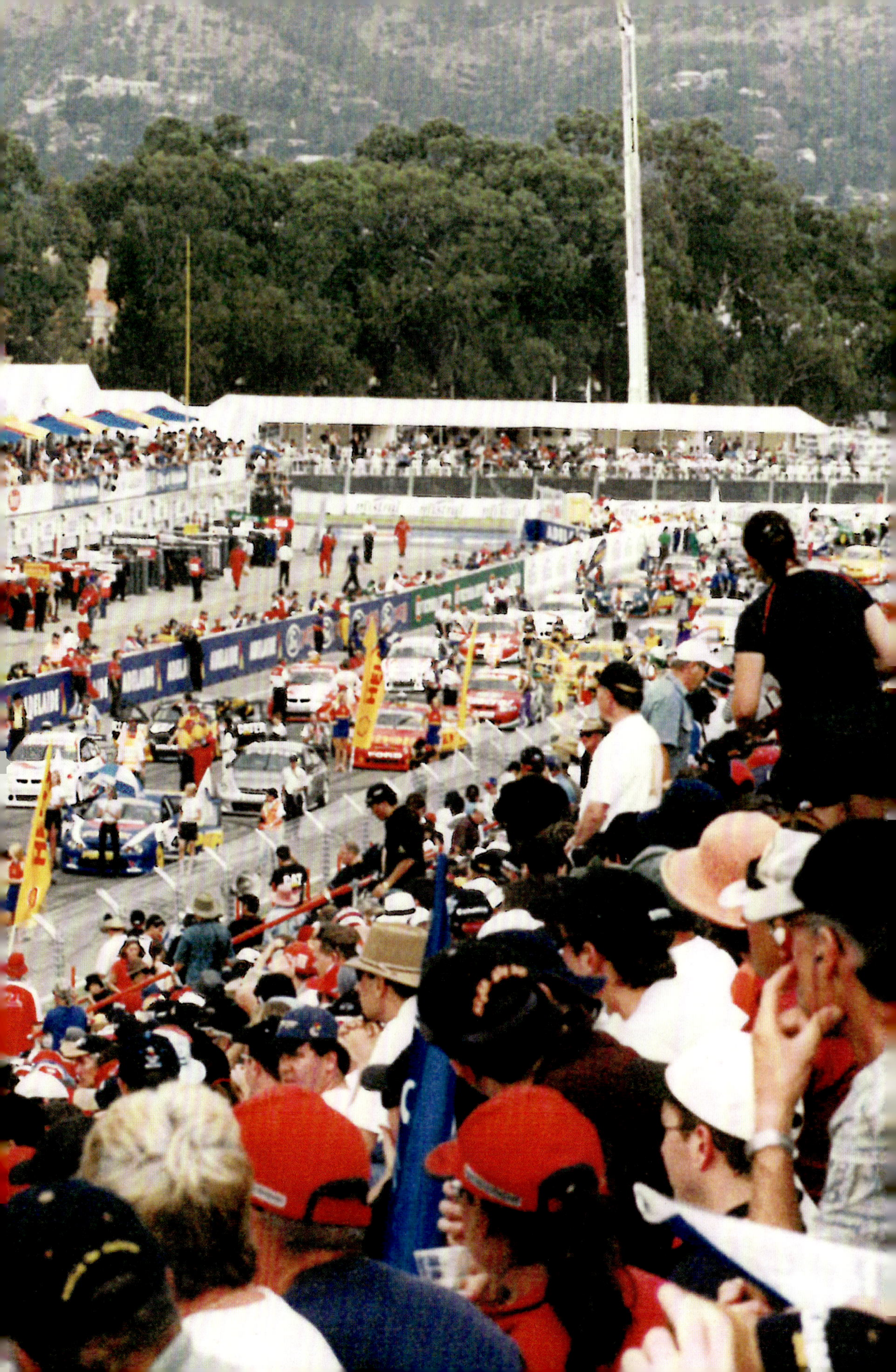
ADELAIDE

IT'S ALL ABOUT COMMITMENT

I always felt I would rather go off the road and ruin a lap that way, by over-committing to it, rather than soft-cocking it and put my foot on the brake too early. Nothing in my world would be as disappointing as putting my foot on the brake on the back straight at Pukekohe half a car length early and making the corner easily. I would be so feral with myself – it would be much worse than if I'd put my foot on the brake two and a half metres too late and run wide.

You've got to be honest with yourself at the end of the day if you want to get the best out of yourself; no-one else would know what you went through. You might look at the raw data and people might say you were slightly early on the brake, but only you would know the real story.

Just put it into perspective: you might have just run a qualifying session and made the top 10 Shootout. You might have had two goes on warm tyres to get yourself to a point of being fast enough to be in the Shootout. So you're organised, you're pretty much up to speed. You then sit around for 15 minutes or half an hour, or sometimes even the whole next day, and now you're sitting in the car and you've got cold tyres. You're going to drive out and both you and the team expect you to put your foot on the brake as deep as you've ever gone, and I can tell you right now, anyone who does that is very good. Your brain's not acclimatised to the speed, it's not acclimatised to the level of grip or the tyre condition or whatever else has changed since you were in the car with everything maximised. You go out and fly down to a corner not knowing whether the car's going to make it or not, and you actually purposely put your foot on the brake so late, so deep and so hard that you think to yourself, *Why did I do that? There's no way it's going to stop*.

You get to the point where you actually scare yourself. Sometimes you get it spot on, other times you could have gone a metre deeper or you needed to be a metre shorter, even if you haven't gone off track. There is absolutely only one person who will know what went on; no data will show what you felt in that moment.

Qualifying in the rain at Pukekohe in 2004 was one of those times we got away with it. We had a shithouse engine and it rained, so our eyes lit up – we thought, 'We're back in it now.' In motorsport if it rains it can often take some of the engine power dramas away, and this was one of those days.

I was fastest in qualifying, but Marcos Ambrose was out before me in the shootout and he did a ripper lap. I went out on my run and it was pissing down. I arrived at turn one – which is fifth gear in the dry and maybe 240km/h – and there were massive puddles of standing water. I turned in and it just bolted on me. It's a big fast right-hand corner, hard on the throttle with full opposite lock and I speedwayed around it because there was no way I was going to give up that easily.

We made it through there and the chicane to get onto the back straight, and the whole way down that I was trying to work out where to brake, while aquaplaning. I had no possible idea because I didn't know how much tyre grip there was, or how wet it was down there, because I hadn't fired at that corner in anger for more than an hour.

So I went blazing down there pulling gears up to 260km/h and I remember when I put my foot on the brake the wheels locked – and when the wheels lock in the rain the engine turns off; it goes silent because the tyres just glide over the wet road. The whole way in I was modulating the brake, trying to make the corner, and by the time I got to the point where I needed to turn the car it was bordering on gone. But I let go of the clutch and the brake and it turned and made the apex and fired straight off the corner. I couldn't believe it. I could have had a hundred goes and wouldn't have got it that good again.

When you're driving really well, all that just happens in slow-mo: the wheels are locked and the car's sliding; you're gathering up and gathering up; and you know the corner's coming so you try to predict the retardation to a point where you say, 'I've got it slow enough now to turn the corner.' The amount of decision-making in that short space of time is just incredible.

So you've done that corner – *phew*, unbelievable. But then you've got to get it out of the corner, you've got to put your foot on the throttle and you don't know how much wheel spin you're going to get; you don't know how much grip you've got. Then it's nice and gentle gear changes to get out of the corner, and then the two fastest corners to finish the lap off.

I remember the tyre bundles on the first of those quick corners and thinking that if I turned it in and slid it, by the time I got there I'd miss the tyres. It worked perfectly. Honestly, another coat of paint would have been enough to have hit the tyres. We got pole by a hundredth of a second, I think, and I remember that lap was absolutely the best I could have possibly driven that car on that day.

It's a very odd sport and that's what makes it great. When I'm being wheeled around the nursing home, that lap and that feeling will live with me forever. When you scare yourself, when it's so wild that you're wondering how you got away with it – that is an amazing feeling.

Above: 2002 Indy.

Top left: 2003 Clipsal.

Top right: 2002 Clipsal.

Bottom left: Early-2000s with Rob Starr, one of my best mates from the HRT era. He was famous for coming on my radio and saying, 'Breathe Mark, breathe'.

Bottom right: 2004 Oran Park.

THE FIERCE COMPETITOR   185

OVERTAKING – A SHORT STORY

You could write a whole book on overtaking. There is so much complexity to it and it really is an art form. There is what I would call simple pass, which comes from the driver in front making an error when you're in the right spot to capitalise. Sometimes things just open up and it works out your way – and you look like a genius and things are good.

But in the main, especially when you're trying to overtake people at the front of the field who don't make many mistakes, it comes from what I call 'constructing the path'. That means that you have to accurately determine whether you've got an advantage over them, and where that advantage is, and then try to position yourself in a way so you can capitalise on it.

It may be that the opponent doesn't come out of a particular corner as well as you do, so once you have worked that out you've then got to work out how to use that advantage. If you are too close, for instance, you might have to lift off and that won't help, so you have to adjust your thinking and break down your strategy.

In any passing move there are essentially two phases: the primary phase is making the move in the first place. Then you've got the secondary phase, which is making it stick. What direction does the next corner go in, and how can I cover a countermove? In essence, if you make a bold move and get on the inside of a corner and then you end up running a little wide to get it done, the other driver can criss-cross and be on the inside for the next corner and take the spot back. It is never a simple equation when you are racing the front of a field like in Australian touring car racing.

If you are driving really well and the car is good, you seem to have more time for thinking and planning these things. But you also have to assess the risk. My passing move on Steven Richards at Bathurst in 2002 just had to be done when it was done; I knew that, with the plastic bag in front of my car, if I parked behind another car I wasn't going to finish. I took the first chance I got and then had to go hard to get some safety between him and me. That was satisfying, but if I didn't get the move done when I did, we wouldn't have finished, let alone have won.

Jason Richards – no relation to Jim or Steven – was another good one at Bathurst in 2005. He was faster across the top of the hill, but we were getting down the hill really well. It meant he'd pull a small gap and then we'd be back on him by the Chase. I knew I needed to get a little closer across the top so I could get a better tow on Conrod, so I worked really hard to get into that position.

Then he made a small mistake at the Elbow. I actually had to give the throttle a little breath not to hit the fence because I was pushing so hard, then I had to tuck in under his wing for the run down the straight. I knew I had to get down the inside of him at the Chase or I was never getting past, so I had to get it all just right at 300km/h. History tells you that I did that; I got past and went on to win the race, but that move took a lot of laps to get right.

Leading Jason Richards at Bathurst in 2005.

AN ICON IN MOTORSPORT'S GOLDEN ERA
Words by John Bowe, former touring car rival

In terms of Motorsport achievements, Skaifey's record is outstanding of course. I first became aware of him in the Laser Series that was quite a hit category in the mid-1980s, but I didn't get to actually meet him until I drove with the Peter Jackson Nissan team in 1987.

He was a young lad then but certainly a character with a well-developed sense of mischief. As he climbed the ladder of Motorsport, he became the quintessential professional, but under the skin is still the same 20-year-old lad! I mean Jack the Lad – if you get my drift! I've enjoyed many laughs with him over the years, and still do although I don't see him as much nowadays.

Mark is very good at getting the right people on his side and being in the right place at the right time, which is a very important skill set in motor racing. I consider the mid-1990s to the mid-2000s to be the pinnacle of touring car racing in this country – and Mark was incredibly successful as a driver then.

He is a great TV commentator too, to be honest, which I guess shows his work ethic in some detail. He is, and always was, a hard worker! Icon is a term used a bit much in racing, but he surely is an icon of Australian motorsport and an engaging and funny bloke to boot.

As a racer, I always thought of him as very fair but hard and tough, which are exactly the ingredients that are needed. I'd love to see him racing again, to be honest, but he's too busy, I guess. Shame though, he would love the TCM.

2003 Phillip Island.

V8 SUPERCARS
AUSTRALIA
DUNLOP
MTAA
SUPER
FUND
Unigraphics
NX
Mobil 1
dodo

CHAPTER 7

THE END OF AN ERA

The last few years of my full-time driving career were among the toughest I can remember. I felt like I was constantly under attack; the structures that had been put in place when I bought HRT were working against us and eventually I just wasn't enjoying what I was doing. We had some great days though in that time – just not enough of them.

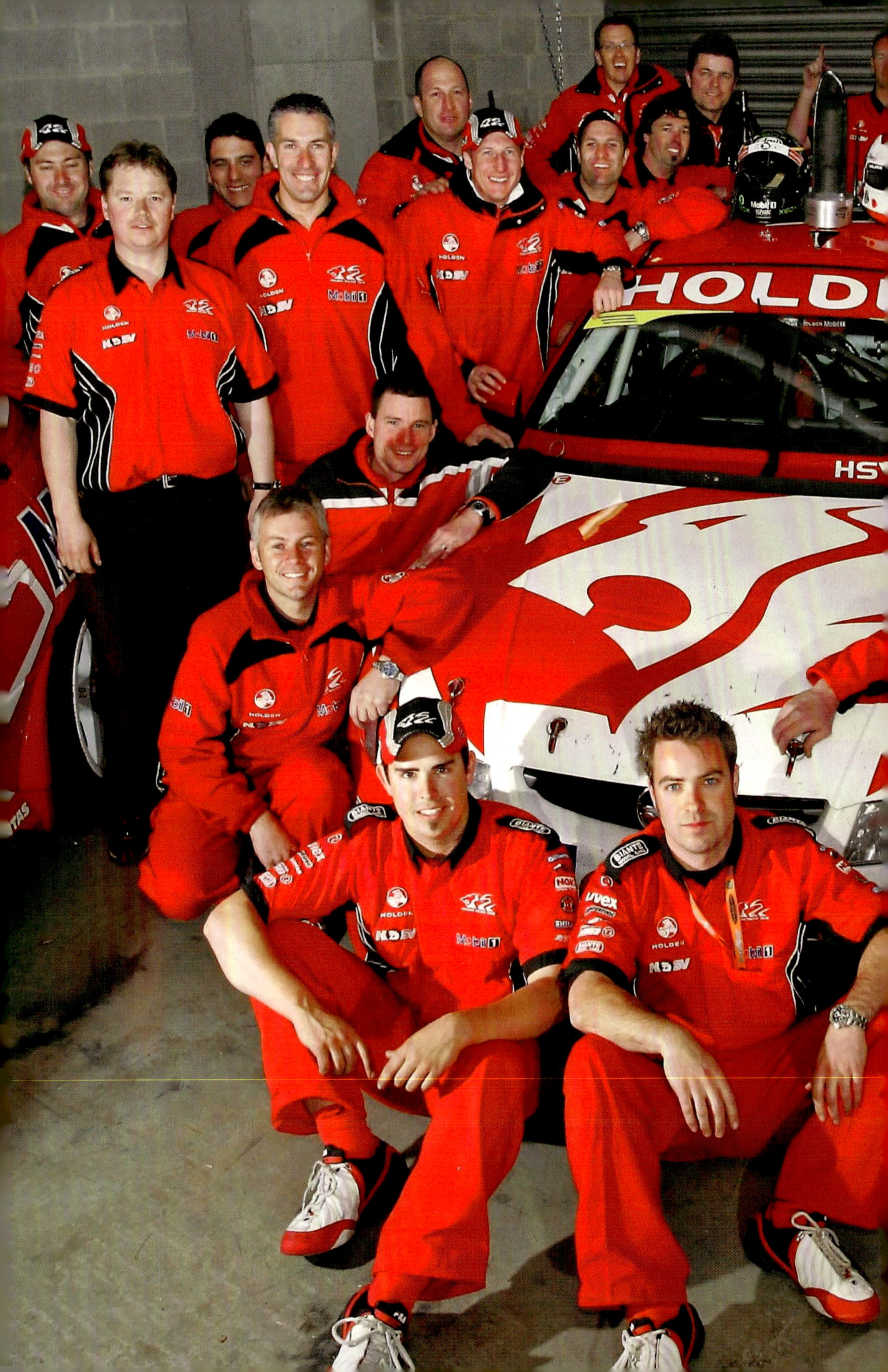
HOLD
HSV
HOLDEN
Mobil 1

Here I am (at driver's door) with co-driver Todd Kelly (at passenger's door) and the rest of the HRT to celebrate our 2005 Bathurst 1000 victory with the winning #2 Commodore VZ. Right behind me with his big claw on my shoulder is Craig Kelly, one of my closest mates who was also CEO of HRT in 2005.

THE END OF AN ERA

HAPPY BIRTHDAY TODD, LET'S WIN BATHURST

Overall we didn't really have a fast enough car in 2005, so we struggled a little at most venues. By the time we got to Bathurst I'd only won two races and Todd Kelly had four in the other car, so mid-season the signs were getting better. It was certainly good for me and Todd to win all three races for our one and only V8 Supercar meeting in China. We'd finished second together at the Sandown 500 and had set our sights on Bathurst as a way to walk away from the season with some positives.

If you remember back, this was the Bathurst with the balaclavas and that big dust up between Ambrose and Murphy, which happened just behind me while I was leading partway through the final stint. This race was a great battle fought against Russell Ingall, Marcos Ambrose, Greg Murphy, Craig Lowndes and Jason Richards, who all had unbelievable pace.

In the third stint it was like a qualifying session. I broke the lap record with 2 minutes and 08.65 seconds and only three other cars did a lap in 2 minutes and 08.00 seconds something that day. I actually did six of them near the end of that stint and I knew we had the speed to win even though it was such a competitive race. That was probably the best stint I have ever done there.

When I was standing there waiting to get into the car for that stint, Robbie Starr came up to me and said, like a footy coach, 'Mate, you've done this before, you know what you've got to do.' It was good though; the car had really come to us through the race. Early on we had too much understeer and too much exit oversteer. As the day went on though, it just got better and better. By the time we got to that pivotal part of the day where you needed to be fastest, we were.

I had to pass Jason early in that last stint and I had to work hard for that. He did make a little mistake and once I got through I had to try putting some distance between us. On that final restart, he was pushing pretty hard, but the car settled after a lap or two and we were in control. I remember coming across the line saying, 'Happy Birthday, mate,' to Todd. We'd managed to win the biggest race of his life on his birthday. I'm not sure anyone else has ever won Bathurst on their birthday – I'm sure someone will tell me if they have – and that just made it a little more special.

Todd joined HRT at the toughest time in its history, back in 2003, and had to watch his younger brother win at Bathurst twice before he got that win. I'm pretty happy for him that we managed to do it that day, and it did soften the blow of what had been a tough year.

En route to victory in the 2005 Bathurst 1000. The win was a record for Holden, marking its seventh straight win in Australia's Great Race.

Greeting the chequered flag at Bathurst in 2005 to seal a fifth Great Race victory. It gave me my third Bathurst win in five years with the HRT, having also won in 2001 and 2002.

MORE THAN A MATE: A BROTHER
Words by Craig Kelly, AFL Premiership player and friend

It all started back in 1989 at a lunch organised by Anne-Maree Sparkman, who was a TV presenter for Nine Network and a mad Collingwood fan. Attendees included Brian Taylor, Tracy Grimshaw, me and this young racing car driver called Mark Skaife.

I was led astray by the driver and missed training that night, but it was the start of a 30-plus year mateship with a friend and confidant who is god father to my second child. A guy who, more than just a mate, is like a brother to me.

One of the most consistent events through this whole journey has been Mark's love for a long lunch or a long chat over plenty of wine and beer. Often these lunches go well into the night and include wrestling, pool games and anything he can do to beat me. He loves the competition.

Mark taught me to drive racing cars around Winton. He and Jim Richards were an amazing team. Fred Gibson gave Mark his first opportunity in Melbourne and as we had both just arrived from interstate around the same time, it allowed us to have a friendship outside of our chosen sports.

When myself and my business partner Rob Woodhouse started our company, Mark allowed us to help and look after him with no track record at all in motorsport, but his desire to assist us was obvious. He not only helped us by allowing us to help him – he also became a great confidant and mentor to me.

Mark's ability and business know-how – outside of racing cars – has placed him in a great position in the Australian sports industry. His ability to phone prime ministers, premiers and CEOs is unparalleled by any other person in the industry. His passion for getting GOONS off the road, making cars safer and making bureaucrats understand the right and wrong way to approach road issues, I believe, has made him the best contributor to road safety in Australia.

He and his wife Toni, the two girls and Mitch, Mark's son, are a wonderful endorsement of how he and Toni manage work and family life. They are a great team and he is a great man. It's wonderful to see many books written about him, as it allows me to be able to hang it on him about how his looks have changed over the years.

The HRT celebrates victory in the 2005 Bathurst 1000 as I sweep past – just moments after taking the chequered flag.

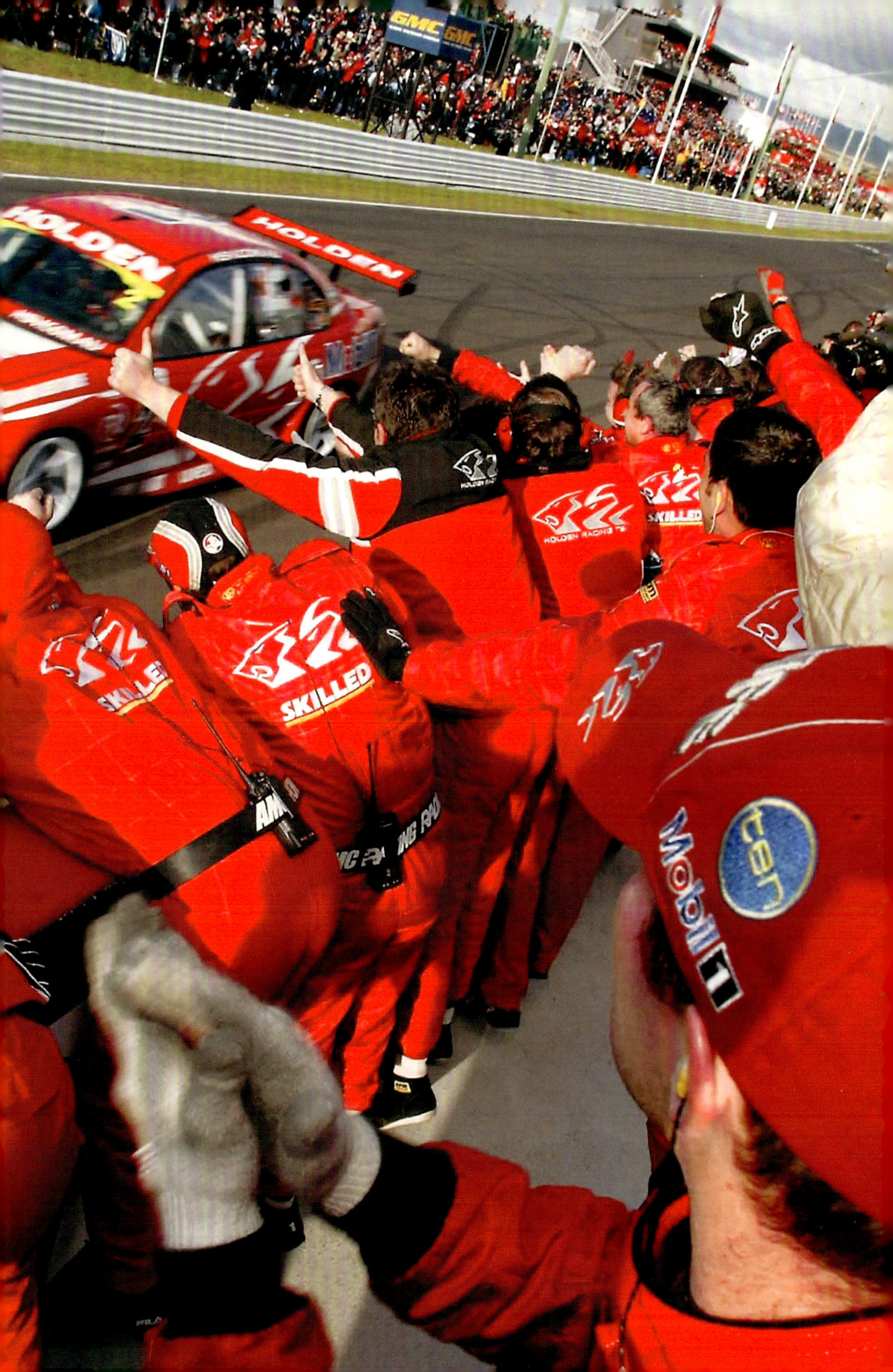
GMC
HOLDEN
HOLDEN
SKILLED
SKILLED
Mobil 1
ten

A GUT-WRENCHING FAILURE

The next year, 2006, was the sort of year I'd rather forget, but I'll never forget that Bathurst. We were the factory Holden team and this was only three or four weeks after Brock had died. It was surreal up there reflecting on one of the great careers in Australian motorsport. We were running a black bonnet that weekend, and for me the only fitting result would be my factory Holden winning the race.

Garth Tander was my co-driver and right from the start of the weekend we were the fastest car. We were consistent – fastest on Thursday, Friday and Saturday – which, given our year, was amazing.

Sitting on the grid, with pole actually being position three because the front row was left vacant in honour of Peter, I can't remember feeling more motivated. Then when I dropped the clutch I knew it was all over; the car barely got off the line and limped around Murrays Corner and onto Mountain Straight, where I got clobbered by Jack Perkins who had no chance to see me when he came out from behind another car.

A day filled with so much promise and we didn't even get a lap done. Then to make matters worse, Jim made one of his rare mistakes at Bathurst and crashed our other car out of the race on lap 24, so there we were with the day all done without even making the first round of pitstops. Marg Curtis, who worked for John Crennan, found us a chopper to get out of Bathurst, and Toni and I were home in time to watch the finish of the race. I was gutted.

But the shit I read after the race was just people trying to stir trouble. It started with this conjecture that I was in third, which was utter rubbish. Then it went through the preparation of the team and saying we were running an experimental clutch and all sorts of other things. It was the same clutch we'd used in 2005. It had been serviced just like all other clutches and should have been fine to do the race. It obviously didn't, but it was just a mechanical failure and that was all.

I am the world's worst loser at the best of times, but on this day it was just too much for me, which is why I bailed. By the time Monday came, I was ready to start doing what I needed to do to get the team back to the top and I started working with Holden to try and make that happen.

Right: With Todd Kelly, who was my HRT teammate for five seasons from 2003 to 2007. Here we are at the Bahrain International Circuit in 2006.

Below: With Todd Kelly and the HRT in the pit lane at the Bahrain International Circuit in 2006.

THE END OF AN ERA   201

Above: 2007 was a year of milestones. I joined the '200' club at Phillip Island when I started my 200th Australian Touring Car/V8 Supercar Championship round. At that point I became just the fifth driver to reach 200 round starts.

Right: Celebrating another milestone victory, this time at Eastern Creek in 2007. That round triumph meant I'd broken the late Peter Brock's record for most round wins in the history of the Australian Touring Car/V8 Supercars Championship.

THE END OF AN ERA

Attacking the fast first corner at Eastern Creek Raceway in Sydney, 2007. In this round I broke Peter Brock's long-time record of most round wins in touring car championship history.

THERE'S A WHOLE OTHER BOOK IN THESE TWO YEARS

You could write an entire book on 2007 and 2008, my last two seasons as a regular driver in the series – and who knows, maybe I will one day. Suffice to say they weren't much fun and I was finding it hard to get up for it each week as the '08 season was winding down.

I remember driving to the track one day for a race and wondering what my daughters were up to, and that is when I knew it was time to give up full-time driving. It is not like you'd look back on my career and think we hadn't achieved; I am immensely proud of my record. It was great to break Brock's record for the most rounds won in the Australian Touring Car Championship at Eastern Creek in 2007, but then the stuff we had to deal with during that period was just draining.

We only ran the Clipsal 500 that year after coming to an agreement with the Touring Car Entrants Group (TEGA) about team ownership, but later we had to formally satisfy the rules relating to control and ownership, which we did because I was the owner and I was in control. I mean, this had been going on for years and it was relentless.

In terms of the racing, Winton in 2007 was one of my worst races ever, but then we got nice bits on the car for Eastern Creek a couple of weeks later and we brained them. It is not like someone comes in and flicks a switch, but for me 2008 was one of my worst seasons – not just in terms of performance, but also enjoyment.

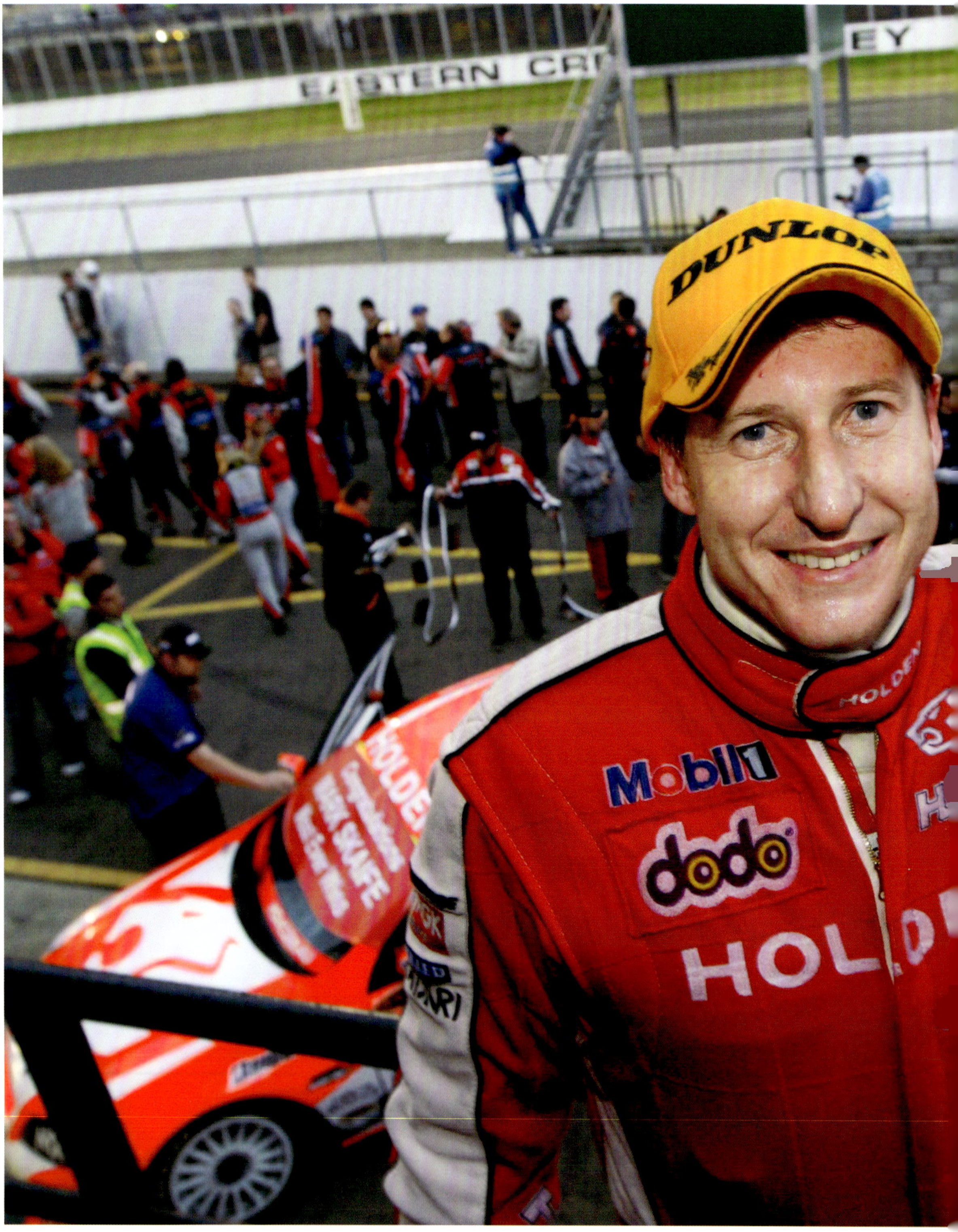
DUNLOP
HOLDEN
Mobil 1
dodo

Celebrating victory in Round 5 of the V8 Supercar Championship Series on the Queen's Birthday Monday in 2007.

Above: Garth Tander and I won the 2008 L&H 500 endurance race at Phillip Island in 2008. It was my last win with the HRT.

Left: Garth Tander and I are introduced to the Bathurst 1000 crowd on race morning in 2008. The race was my 12th and final Bathurst start with the HRT.

By the time Oran Park came at the end of the season, I was pretty much done. I'd looked at joining forces with Larry Perkins at one stage, but that wasn't going to work, so I knew I had one of two choices. I either had to buy Tom out of Holden Motorsport, or I needed to sell to him. Not long after the final round, having effectively retired as a full-time driver, I chose the latter. It was real heart-versus-head stuff, and the decision was hard because of the reasons I bought in the first place, but I am confident even to this day it was the right thing to do.

Oran Park in 2008 was a fantastic weekend and a great track for me to say goodbye to the series as a full-time driver. The track had meant so much to me when I was growing up, so it was a fitting place for my finale and everyone – the Setons and Tony Perich at Oran Park, Tony Cochrane at V8 Supercars and the team at Seven Network – did an amazing job.

There was a great presentation on the main straight and the lap on the back of the ute was fantastic. The crowd was just amazing, and even the people who had booed when I was at Nissan, or the Ford fans that didn't like me when I was at Holden were awesome. Lindsay Fox flew his private plane up with all my best mates from Melbourne and my mates from Wyong came down and enjoyed a hospitality tent that was set up for them.

My daughters Mia and Tilly aren't old enough to remember much of it, but it was special to have them there. Mitch was with Toni for most of the day. He was 13 at the time and I think he'll remember that day as fondly as I do.

Honestly, I was just blown away. The reaction was fantastic. That sort of response gives you faith that the people really do understand what we do and why we do it, and in reverse, you understand what sort of role you play in both sport and entertainment. It made it all seem worthwhile and I can't thank the people who turned up that day enough for how they treated me.

THE END OF AN ERA

THIRTY YEARS OF GETTING 'SKAIFED'
Words by Mark Larkham, former racing rival and current TV teammate

I'll say little about Mark the race driver – I'm just not going there. I lived nearly the entire period, and like so many was punished by it. As Crompo regularly and beautifully articulates on the matter with a (high-pitched) 'zzzzzzzzzzzzzzzzzzzz – you know the feeling of the dentist's drill?' ..'nuff said.

I will say Mark was a true champion in the driver's seat, and worked harder to achieve that (and still does) than most will ever realise. Exactly like Schumacher, Mark was never just a driver in the team, he drove the team.

We've been around each other one way or another for around 30 years now. During our Formula Brabham days in the early-90s he was definitely my 'nemesis', and then we battled to a (lesser) degree in Supercars. But we have turned out to be the closest of mates, and right up front, I love the guy, as a true mate. I don't give a crap who he is in public life.

In fact, I now know that as a public racing figure, Mark was perhaps judged too harshly in that love or hate Holden/Ford pub yarn. Yes, he was sometimes brutal in the application of his tenacity, control of the detail, and his 'do all things necessary' approach. But I can assure you after maturing in the industry with him for three decades, the kinds of words that summarise the lesser known character that I have grown to love are: fun, generosity, laughter, warmth, integrity, humility, kindness, family and most of all, mateship. He really does characterise what a true Aussie mate means.

Why nemesis? We were well prepared, but Mark (including Freddy and his great team) 100% got in the way of any chance I had of bagging an Australian Drivers' Championship in those years (twice). It was also the time I started to note why Mark was constantly on the pace, because he had his finger well and truly on the pulse; he was more than a driver. The attention to detail, the engineering understanding, the relentless vigour and front-footed attitude were there for all to see, and for me to study in his endless pursuit of success.

Crompo (who also raced Formula Brabham) and I still laugh about the difference between Skaifey and the two of us. Maybe the reason his trophy cabinet has more silverware than ours is he would sell his grandmother to get better anti-roll bar bushes and we would, well, just lease her out.

Above: Leading fellow Commodore drivers Cameron McConville and Jason Richards at Oran Park in 2008.

Right: This was my final appearance as a full-time V8 Supercar driver. A huge crowd came out to Oran Park in Sydney in 2008 for the final round of that year's Championship. It was an appropriate venue to finish my full-time career given I'd won more races there (15) than at any other track in my Australian Touring Car/V8 Supercar Championship career.

THE END OF AN ERA   211

While there was a healthy rivalry between us in Formula Brabham, which I could only recreate once or twice in the next decade in Supercars as Mark continued to succeed, there was quite a degree of angst and animosity between us in meeting rooms too. We represented our respective manufacturers at the variety of board tables and technical committees and discussions during 1996–2006, the decade of enormous growth of the sport predominately under Tony Cochrane's vision. The stakes were high, and they were rising.

For much of that period in the blue corner were Dick Johnson and myself, while Mark was always prominent on the other side. In those AVESCO and TEGA board years, Garry Rogers on the Holden side was a breath of fresh air – still tough, but approximately 1000% less intense than HRT's Skaife, Crenno and Grech. With significant manufacturer support, and no doubt pressure, coupled to the sheer competitive win-at-all-cost attitude that was part of HRT's and Mark's DNA, well, the going got tough at times.

Remember, coming from previous decades of a variety of cars and classes, these were the days of intense parity debates and politicking that make today's squabbles, important as they are, timid by comparison.

Manufacturer money was spread across many teams back then, so the fighting and frustration was intense, but just like today, Mark always came prepared, took notes, stayed ahead of the information curve, carefully influenced the agenda and stood his ground on heated debates – no matter how heated.

With strong support from Larry Perkins, John Crennan and Mark in particular had to battle hard as cost control and increased 'unpredictability of result' measures were pushed into the category. Most of them would impact their team and its success more than any other – control ECU, control tyres, and then of course Project Blueprint, which has underpinned the pathway for nearly two decades.

In fact, I remember Mark unpacking a box and plonking a new Holden Supercar cylinder head design among the paperwork on the board table – such was his preparedness to make his point and win the argument ... commendable. Yet even with all the intensity, MS would never lose his lot or throw a hissy fit, always respectful. It was kinda like across the table I was the clear opponent, but never the enemy – an important distinction.

Under the strong tutorage of Crennan, Mark played hardball, as did Crennan, and just as he should have, given the unprecedented link that had been formed between the success of Holden's racing operation and its vehicle sales, particularly the aspirational HSV brand in which Mark figured heavily. I reckon even today Mark could name most of the dealer principals of Holden Dealerships across the country. But what I always truly admired was that once the fight was over, won or lost, Mark had the ability to move straight to 'what is best for the sport' mode – you know, best outcome. I reckon he was scored pretty hard in this period. Not many, or not enough saw this side. I did.

Mark loves the sport, genuinely loves the sport. From the business, commercial, even the political, right through to having a great understanding of race car dynamics and the role of the rebound shim sitting in a digressive shock absorber piston stack. I can count on one hand those that have this breadth of knowledge.

But it is his competitiveness that sets him apart; I've seen it for 30 years. I've seen it at the track, I've seen it at the board table and I've seen it at the bar – Mark doesn't suffer fools and there has been more than the odd time where less-wise Mark (me) says to more-wise Mark, 'C'mon mate, home time!'

The dynamic between Mark, Neil and myself has been a highlight of our personal and professional lives post racing. The chemistry you see is real, our mateship is real, and in the TV workspace it all connects so well, including the others in our team. The deep desire for success has simply spilt into the TV world, the pursuit of 'improving the product' never ends and we see that same professional detail Skaifey applied to racing in the same size-three font notes he accumulates all day long.

We were all in the car heading to Darwin's circuit for a Supercar race two years ago – 'Mark, Mark and Neil' (as we call ourselves and as a crow would articulate). Enjoyable as the car trip always is, it was a bit of Groundhog Day, so we did a calculation as to just how much time we had collectively spent at a racetrack, using our good mate, former engineer and numbers man Oscar Fiorinotto, who was with us. We arrived at an insane amount of time – I can't recall the exact number but it was years and years.

My point being, a big chunk of my motor racing life has been with Mark. As competitors, as competing board and technical committee members (Ford and Holden), and now as close mates – what a journey.

Money didn't get Mark where he is; his competitive instinct and deep desire for success did, so he earned his spot on the touring car grid. As such, even as fierce competitors in Formula Brabham, he kind of 'had my back' as I entered the Touring

With former racer, and also turned TV analyst, Mark Larkham at Bathurst in 2009 for the launch of my illustrated race history book – written by Andrew Clarke, who helped me with this book too. At this stage I was still blending my commentary work with racing in the enduros.

THE END OF AN ERA 215

Car Championship a couple of years later, no doubt as a consequence of the solid professional respect we had developed in the open wheelers. So, as has been well documented, my team and I built a car to enter touring cars in 1995 that was way over engineered, more like an open wheeler, and it failed. So those early years we were lost, as Skaifey was enjoying success in his Commodores up the front of the grid.

It was hard to turn to any competitor for genuine believable advice. But it was Mark who actually reached out and offered help, and such was the competitive bond and respect we shared in Formula Brabham. He asked me to send him some figures/detail and he responded with detailed drawings, figures and concepts as to what he and his engineers thought we should do. I still have those documents, mostly hand drawn by Mark, such was the gravity of what they meant to me.

That was the turning point that broke through a professional relationship and cemented a bond as friends living and surviving in the same industry. That in turn developed into a meaningful friendship, and then the 10 odd years we have spent together in TV away from the driving seat has ensured true mateship – we will be tight for life.

And over those hundreds of meals and all the drinking, we have laughed hard, laughed often and laughed loud, constantly mischievous and cheeky, walking right up to the line, doing our best not to step over it. We call it getting 'Skaifed' and it can be evidenced clearly on my credit card statements, the balance of which ebbs and flows perfectly in line with the Supercar calendar!

One of my favourites was at Townsville about five years back. We'd been dining in the Casino restaurant where we were staying and it was getting late, but we had our 'naughty boy' hats on. The night was getting on and we were ready for some fine wine ('wise' Mark doesn't drink 'un-fine' wine). Sadly, the quality wine cabinet had been locked, the manager had left and we weren't having any of that.

So Mark (whose celebrity the waiter had no idea of) piped up with, 'You may have heard of us – Mark & Mark Locksmiths?' So I quickly grabbed a dessert spoon, two knives and a fork, and we approached this rather significant, well-locked glass cabinet. By now the entire restaurant (mostly race fans there for the event) were onto it. Of course, we broke through to the delight and cheer of the crowd – 'Wine bar's open!' It was like we were straight out the back streets of the suburbs. Fact is, we both are, and it's a great connector for us.

I often use Mark as an example when motivating young drivers – a boy from a

Wyong tyre shop that made it his business to become a champion, and then made it his business to climb higher after that. He doesn't stop, and his career is far from finished.

For all of that, Mark's most impressive quality is that he never lost sight of where he came from. He's still the boy from Wyong who grew up in and around his dad's tyre business, and all of the rough, tumble and vigour that stood for in the early 1980s – a kinda 'boys' club' on steroids. Mark has made it his business to intentionally learn, adapt, and evolve into what he needed to be to succeed. His dad Russell is a 'ripping good bloke' (as MS would say) and is a big part of Mark's humanity, humility and the great Aussie larrikin that lurks within, which was for many years hidden behind his steely industry profile. Russell also doesn't suffer fools and passed that gene to Mark. I'd suggest that Russell has dropped more than the odd wanker on his arse.

MS can have a beer-swilling, cussing, swearing, laugh-out-loud pub session with the best of them, and then flick a switch and host a senior government or industry dinner with all the pomp, grandeur and vocabulary required. He makes it his business to be across industry knowledge and the daily news cycle and can deliver in that environment with the best of them – but it's all real. It is a very impressive quality, and should serve as inspiration to others looking to succeed in our commercialised world. He worked and chose to make himself that person.

For all the piss-taking I do about the moths in his wallet, it is exactly the opposite – he is in fact one of the most generous people I know. We have eaten at restaurants hundreds of times over the years and drunk a minimum of three Warragambas of alcohol – but the pay-tab ratio is well in his favour. Not at all because of wealth, and not because I/we don't offer and argue over who pays, but because it is evident across so much of Mark's social and personal life, he is generous at heart, he genuinely enjoys giving. ◉

I WASN'T DOING A BROCK, BUT IT WASN'T OVER

When I decided to walk away from everything, I needed to know what I was going to do. I asked John Crennan to get involved with that. I think at that time he knew me as well as anyone, and as I've said elsewhere, he was so smart I thought he could help me. He prepared a document called *Life After Driving,* which formed a big part of the 'Skaife Next' plan: a document that was about 80 pages long and laid out a plan for everything. There was a plan for the media, engineering and track design (which was probably the bit he got a little wrong – it has turned out bigger than we thought) and other business opportunities that I explored with a group I call the Life Committee, headed by David White and Craig Kelly.

With John's booklet, they helped me map it all out. In 2009 I landed a role as co-commentator for V8 Supercars with Seven Network, just after I retired from full-time racing. But even with that going on, I wanted to get some endurance drives done and see if I could win Bathurst again. James Henderson and Tim Miles were part of the Tasman ownership group, under which James and I thrashed out a commercial deal to join the team and the endurance races. Jeff Grech, who had worked with me early on at HRT, was running the Tasman Motorsport team with Greg Murphy as his lead driver, and I joined them in 2009 after negotiating a deal with Seven Network to release me from commentary for the enduros.

That Bathurst would go down as one of the saddest misses for me. We had the fastest car and we pretty much had an eight-second lead over the eventual winners because of our strategy, but Murph had just passed the pit entry when he was called in because a Safety Car was coming out. It was that close; if he'd made the pits we would have won, no doubt. It was a tough day and we worked hard to be in that position. I did a spell in the middle of that race on cold tyres that I just couldn't get up to temperature on the wet track and it was just shocking. I thought I was going to crash more than a dozen times, and when the tyres came off at the end of the stint they wouldn't have been much warmer than ambient.

Safety cars work for you some days and they kill you on others. This was a day they didn't work for us, and we knew when Murph missed pit lane it was all over. We ended up fourth and an HRT car won, so that was a tough day, although I was happy for the guys in the team.

My first weekend racing with Team Vodafone and Craig Lowndes brought instant success as we claimed victory in the 2010 L&H 500 at Phillip Island. It came 10 years after our last race win together – the 2000 Queensland 500 endurance race during our time as teammates at the HRT.

THREE OUT OF FOUR AIN'T BAD

After running Bathurst with Murph in 2009, Roland Dane from Triple Eight rang me to see if I wanted to drive with Craig Lowndes in the endurances races, which sounded like a good idea to me.

For two blokes – Roland and me – who you would think A) wouldn't get on, and B) would be hard to deal with, we actually made the deal happen very simply. We've both done the odd contract in our motorsport lives, and this time we didn't even run it through lawyers. He basically sent me an agreement, I sent him back some comments, he came back with another one and after three or four email exchanges we ticked it off and signed the deal. I know it's only 10 years ago, but to be able to do an agreement 10 years ago without having a legal representative on either side, and to do that deal without falling out of love, is a bit unheard of. So that was a good start.

It's very similar in some ways to the deal I did with Brock for his last race for us. I sat down with Peter, and I remember very clearly saying, 'At the end of this, PB, we're going to be mates. If you do mad commercial deals or things that are outside the team's best interests, or aren't endorsed by the team, we will fall out of love.' I had that as a face-to-face conversation with him, and he was absolutely superb. Not a single drama.

When I think about my time with Roland's team, not only did I gravitate to and become very close with the engineering group, but Roland and I also never had a bad word. Everybody did their job; it was really professional and it was thoroughly enjoyable.

We got a bit unlucky with that second Bathurst. If you look back now you can see how we were hurt by double stacking and other circumstances. We could have easily won four races from the four starts, but the record books have it as three from four with a second place, so all of them were on the podium which was still a great outcome. The first win was the L&H 500 at Phillip Island, and then we backed that up with the 2010 Supercheap Auto Bathurst 1000 – my sixth win there. But that was not an easy race. We'd worked hard to develop a good race car and when I was injured during the race, having such a good car proved critical when Craig had to triple stint at the end.

Popping that rib out is the most painful thing I have ever experienced – even worse than the bucket-handle rib dislocation of 1991 – and it happened so quickly and innocuously. Basically, I turned the maximum amount of steering lock at the Dipper, and as I came off the Dipper it landed hard and it popped the rib out from the pressure, or the impact with the seat. I couldn't breathe, and when we pitted three laps later I was battling to get out of the car. Craig actually had to drag me out, and then when I was battling for breath, I said to Chris Brady – the physio at Triple Eight – that I didn't think I could get back in. We did everything we could to put the rib back in place, and my God if I was sore before, that was nothing on this. We taped it up just in case, but I wasn't needed. Craig put in an extraordinary drive and we won the race from our teammates Jamie Whincup and Steve Owen.

Lowndsey and I had been really tough competitors up until these races, but we'd also become good mates over time. We had some classic battles, and some inter-team rivalries that made them even bigger. If you think about my time at HRT, I drove Bathurst with him in 1998, so this was almost like coming full circle. Many people probably didn't think that we were that friendly, but the reality is we've always had a really high respect for each other.

I was working very hard on making it a nice race car, and Craig drove it well in qualifying and the race. We were very compatible and we always have been that way. People think we drive the cars very differently, and yes, there are some technique differences, but it's not like we can't drive each other's package, or can't slightly compromise. But we didn't really have to, to be honest; the car was pretty much to both of our likings. The ergonomics were easy, the set-up of the car was effective, the team was ultra-professional and we got on with life. There was no drama.

I was playing my role – I knew what I had to do and I did it. It wasn't as hard as I thought, running as a co-driver, because I was focused on the job at hand. The second year was just as fulfilling as the first, although winning Bathurst would have made it even sweeter.

My role off the track with Supercars was becoming more complex, so I just stepped away from racing after Bathurst in 2011 with no fanfare or anything – I just stopped. I'd been working with Roland, Tony Cochrane (who ran V8 Supercars) and Tim Miles, who was a sales agent for the sport. We were

vodafone
NOKIA
Standard 8856-2000
RS.161.08
REVOLUTION
Year of manufacture: 2010
Crescent

With Craig Lowndes after our victory in the 2010 L&H 500 at Phillip Island.

224   MARK SKAIFE

Celebrating on the podium after the Phillip Island win.

THE END OF AN ERA

effectively selling Supercars. SEL was selling its share entirely and the teams were selling down, dropping their equity stake from 75% to 40 or 35% in what was called Project Tazio.

We were heavily engaged with people everywhere while buying this large chunk of Supercars. It was a mountain of work and a lot of presentations. We were selling blue sky and we were fully engaged with a lot of different parties. The sport was going very well – it was making good money at around $35 million profit a year, but we were also selling a set of circumstances and a roadmap for making more money than that. We had a few interested parties and in the end a deal was done with Archer Capital.

The restructure of the business had a V8 Supercars Commission and I was to become the inaugural Commission Chairman. For me, that meant I had to step away from the racing, because I felt it was a conflict, or at least could have raised concerns over conflicts.

I was also working pretty hard on the Car of the Future development, and that was a massive job in itself, but that too I think required me to be independent. So with a 75% win rate with Triple Eight, I just stopped racing and I have never regretted that. It was the right time for me to do it.

Conferring with then-V8 Supercars CEO Martin Whittaker at Bathurst in 2010.

WE WENT OUT AND WENT *BANG*
Words by Craig Lowndes, racing driver and former teammate

In 2010, a decade since I had last shared a ride with Mark back when we were in Holdens, Roland rang to tell me we were going to try and get him on board for the endurance races. Roland had tried earlier when we were running Fords, but that was never going to happen. This time though it did, and I was very much in favour of it happening.

I knew we could drive together; he had heaps of experience and I thought he could help. When I broke Murph's lap record at Bathurst that was literally off the back of the session before, which Mark had used to set up the car. I went out in it and went *bang* and broke the lap record.

We had three wins from our four races together, and this includes a Bathurst win. We worked hand in hand and we still do today in the sense of me joining the commentary team. I think it is because we respect each other; we don't have any egos in the sense of trying to beat each other. We just work really well together as a team. So, to get that team back together was quite ingenious of Roland at the time.

When we won Bathurst in 2010, I had to do a triple stint because Mark popped a rib out. What happened was, because of his short torso he'd loosened the belts a little to get more leverage, and on one lap in the Dipper the car dropped and bottomed out and he didn't go with it straight away, and when he did, he landed on the wing of the seat.

He finished the stint, but once he was out of the car that was it, he physically couldn't get back in the car. But he didn't hide it, his ego didn't get in the way of the team. The result was fantastic because we ended up winning. I gave him the biggest hug when he made it down to the podium, and I remember him just taking a big breath and wincing because of the pain.

Above: I returned to TeamVodafone for 2011, again teaming to drive with Craig Lowndes. Here I watch the action from the pits at Phillip Island.

Right: Craig Lowndes and I backed up our Phillip Island 500 victory from 2010 a year later. Added to victory at Bathurst in 2010, the win in the 2011 Phillip Island race gave us three endurance race wins in a row.

DUNLOP
DUNLOP
20
HOLDEN
KOMATSU
CALTEX
vodafone
Norton by Symantec
TOSHIBA
vodafone
NOKIA

SKAIFEY – FROM ENEMIES TO FRIENDS!
Words by Roland Dane, team owner at Triple Eight Race Engineering

From the moment that Triple Eight set foot on track in V8 Supercars at Sandown 2003, Mark and the Holden Racing Team were the number one enemy! And that was purely because he was the benchmark driver at the benchmark team, and we had to beat them if we were going to win races and championships, plus Bathurst.

When you fight someone hard and they fight back hard, then respect is bred even if you still hate each other. It is hard to beat someone in this sport if you like them, but you can respect them. And so, my relationship with Mark was built on respect as fierce competitors right through until he retired from full-time driving. I wasn't alone in having this kind of relationship with him – as I also wasn't alone in then being able to develop a very different relationship once he'd stepped away from the Holden Racing Team.

And so, in late 2009, after some teams had got fed up with us fielding the Whincup/Lowndes combination at Bathurst each year, when the driver rules changed for the Endurance races to stop the combining of two full time drivers into one car, I approached Mark to ask whether he'd be interested in pairing up with Craig. It took us a total of about three emails to get the deal done! Cue calls from all and sundry asking me why I'd let myself in for all the 'baggage' that would accompany Mark once we went testing and racing. I can honestly say that we never saw any of that in the two seasons he raced with us. The #888 car was engineered by Jeromy Moore and, in the four races Skaifey did with us, the CL/MS combination won three and came second once (losing the 2011 Bathurst win by 0.29 of a second). A pretty bloody good record by anyone's standards!

The fact is that Mark turned up, let us do our job and got on and did his – exactly what we'd asked for – and proved himself to be a great operator. He formed friendships within the Triple Eight team that remain to this day and rebuilt his relationship with Craig as they became teammates again after a ten-year hiatus. The Dream Team in the #888 car was formed from a rule change that the people who'd instigated it hadn't thought through, as they hadn't foreseen that we'd get together with our previous nemesis. Along the way, we showed that you can never ignore one of motor racing's oldest sayings: never say never!

Skaifey is rightly an icon of Australian motorsport and a good mate – but more than anything else, I respect Mark as the fiercest competitor that I have encountered in the sport. He hates losing as much as I do!

MY MATE, STUPE
Words by John Elsworth, former Director at Holden

I first met Skaifey about 20 years ago when I was the Head of Marketing for Holden, and I recall hitting it off really well. Similar age. Similar sense of humour. Similar love for cars. Similar enjoyment of icy cold beer.

We have a friendship that has stood the test of time. We've celebrated sporting wins, business success, kids, birthdays and weddings over the journey.

We have a mutual respect and have actually called each other 'Stupe' (that's short for 'Stupid') for years. Some people may find that odd to have such a self-deprecating (shared) nickname, however, I think it's our way of keeping each other's feet planted, not allowing each other to get ahead of ourselves and not taking each other too seriously.

While I truly admired Stupe's achievements on the racetrack, I have long admired his achievements post-racing. I recall having some conversations with him when he was considering retiring from racing. It is a really difficult period for sporting heroes when they're confronted with the 'What am I going to do next?' scenario. We discussed how he could keep doing the things he loved and being involved in the car game in some form – whether it was through commentary, operations for race events, journalism or even becoming a car dealer. (Although I think I put a dampener on that when I told him how little the margins are and that they're open seven days a week.)

Throughout my time at Holden, Stupe was retained for many things – customer drive events, product launches, dealer events and plenty of advertising, and I knew the 'Hey Skaifey' Commodore ads were working when he rang me to tell me he was tired of blokes yelling out 'Hey Skaifey' whenever he was out and about. On every occasion we utilised his services, Stupe was the consummate pro.

But there's one thing that has always stood out for me. In 2012 I decided to leave Holden (after 22 years) for a rival car company. At the time I was the Head of Sales, Marketing and Aftersales for Holden, and when you're in a leadership position, it can be a lonely place. Sometimes you wonder whether people befriend you because of your role rather than you as a person. It was terrifying … would anyone still talk to me once my move was announced? Well, my fears quickly evaporated when the first phone call I received was from Stupe. He offered an ear, his understanding, his support, and his friendship.

Stupe – a champion on the racetrack. Champion businessman. Champion family man. Champion mate.

Presenting to the media and industry at Sydney Olympic Park Pavilion on the Car of the Future.

CHAPTER 8

LIFE AFTER RACING

When the racing finally stopped totally, it was time to put the 'Skaife Next' plan into action. Today, I have a whole bunch of new teams and people I consider family, and I love what I do.

MY NEW TEAM

I cannot speak highly enough of the team at Fox Sports and the amount of effort and mateship that goes into making a telecast or another TV show. Like in my early days at Seven with Simon Fordham and Nathan Prendergast, we just work at getting the right people into the right role and then go about making the most informative and entertaining show we can, like how the *Supercars Sidetracked* show came about when the sport shut down for Coronavirus. I'd wanted to do something like that for a while, and when we spoke about it as a team it came together pretty quickly.

I do miss the hardcore intensity of driving and racing at the highest level, but when that red light comes on and you are live on air, there's a level of pressure and expectation that is the closest thing I can ever imagine to being with a racing team.

People don't understand the level of work that goes on in the background to make the shows. Yes, there is a lot of piss-taking and laughing and joking going on, but there's a serious narrative of telling the story of a particular weekend. We've got what we call the Ten Commandments: the ten serious things that we have to cover every weekend. We really mark ourselves on whether we've actually been able to convey these or not.

Take this little snapshot: when Neil Crompton and I call a race, we have to know what is happening with 24 cars – where in the past I've only needed to worry about one or two. We are monitoring the pit-to-driver radio for all those cars and keeping track of what is going on with all of them. We've got all these screens with vision and data and a range of commercial imperatives to meet – corner sponsors, replay sponsors … when is the ad break? In the background of that, and in our other ear we've got a Nathan Prendergast or David Tunnicliffe or someone else giving us directions, and every man and his dog, from Larry Perkins and Allan Moffat to the PRs from teams, texting in information.

You could be in the middle of a sentence while someone in the truck is giving you directions about what you are going to do in 10 seconds … so you try to wrap up the story before you get the three-two-one. People sit back and say, 'Gee, they missed that!' and we probably have. Sometimes I look at the results and wonder how someone got to where they finished. There's so much stuff going on.

Neil and I were really good mates before we started doing TV together, but we're seriously hard on each other and hard on ourselves as a consequence, because we both want to do a really good job. And that's part of a new family for me. I didn't even know Jess Yates when this whole thing started, but she is a serious journo and she works bloody hard. She's just been fantastic and she sees it all through a different lens, which gives the telecast great perspective. Neil, Mark Larkham, Greg Murphy and I are hardcore motor racing people, so she is often a balance to that and comes at it from a broader sport journalism perspective.

You also wouldn't believe how much work Larko does with his things. Those drawings and ideas are fantastic, and how he tells the story adds so much to the telecast. But if he wasn't fascinated with things and didn't do the research, then you'd know, because it wouldn't come across so well. God knows how much time he's spent on each of those six-minute things on *Sidetracked*.

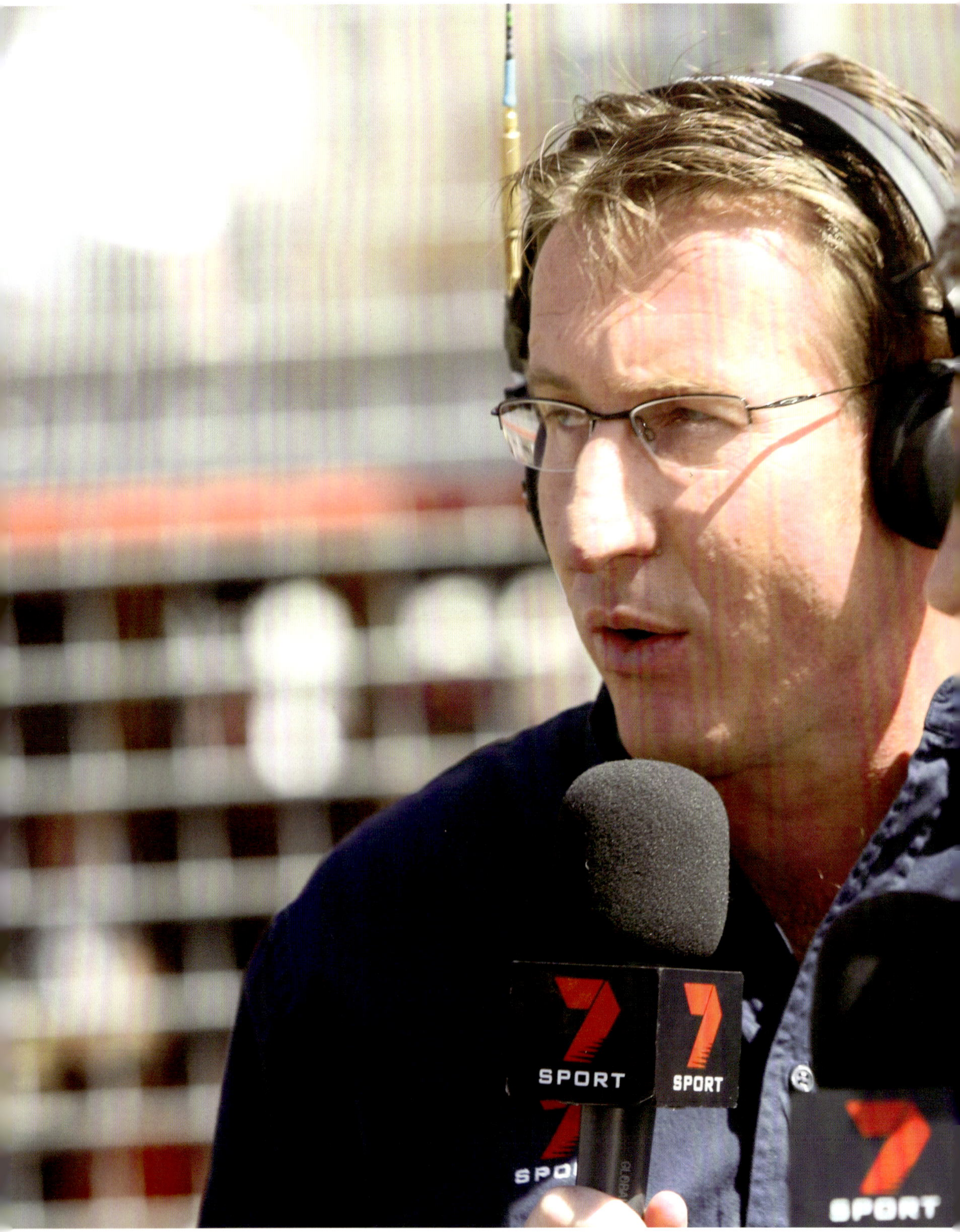
7
SPORT
7
SPORT
7
SPORT

I made the move into television in 2009 after my full-time V8 Supercar career ended. Here I'm with Neil Crompton presenting to camera at that year's Clipsal 500 in Adelaide.

LIFE AFTER RACING 237

'YOU BLOKES MUST BE KIDDING YOURSELVES...'
Words by Neil Crompton, former racing teammate, current TV teammate

Skaifey? Frankly, he's a giant pain in the backside and has been for 35 years. These introductions are meant to be glowing, warm and syrupy but the truth is way more entertaining!

We're live, I'm wide-eyed, frozen stupid in the grip of on-camera terror; I am metaphorically sweating bullets in the cold Mount Panorama night air and cannot remember the name of the bloody TV show!

'Welcome back to – errr [dead air] it's ah ... [more dead air] ... [bigger blank stare down the lens and even more dead air] ...' Nice work.

The situation-saving contribution made by the goon next to me (aka the co-host, Mark Skaife OAM) is to merely chuckle like Mutley from the *Whacky Races* cartoon, laughing so much internally his shoulders are bouncing up and down like clapped-out shock absorbers on a corrugated country road. He didn't look sideways at his now desperate, panicked mate – not for an eye blink. He looked straight ahead ... this was the TV equivalent of me locking all four brakes and hitting the fence. Hard. All on national television. He loved it.

Time and place? Friday 5 October 2012. Live on air, Seven Network, the annual light-hearted preview to the Great Race, was it *Pit Lane Live* or *Friday Night Live*? Didn't know then, dunno now. We were in a golden career period, making all kinds of shows. Which one was this?

It's just one of hundreds, maybe thousands of similar scenes that have unfolded in locations around Australia and various parts of the motorsport-loving universe. These include driver briefings, bars, commentary boxes, host sets, engineering debriefs, radio station studios, restaurants, start lines, shopping centres, car dealerships, sponsor gigs ... sometimes all in one day.

That's right – three and a half decades and counting ... it's a lifetime, perhaps better described as a life sentence! Yes, as a matter of pure fact, I have enjoyed an access-all-areas, front-row seat to the successful life and times of Mark Stephen Skaife.

Getting to the point. With MS, you're either a flog or not. Most of the time, I've remained in the latter group. What you see is what you get. Mark is no-nonsense.

Candour is always in copious supply. In the brutal world of professional motor racing, this is a pre-requisite. At dinner: he's a funny, engaging raconteur. In his natural habitat, the cockpit: ruthlessly focused on steering a racing car into absolute submission en route to even more success.

The record is impressive. For his mates like Mark Larkham and myself, we were banished into what felt like a decade in the results wilderness.

Oh, and those poor cars along the way ... the Ford Laser, Nissan Skyline, Nissan GT-R, SPA or Lola Formula Holden, Holden Commodore, each machine eventually submitted to his skill and/or his sheer brute force.

Many images remain etched in my mind and will remain for life. Like millions of Australians, I recall the many triumphs and the odd hiccup. However, when you dissect this bloke, his career, his reign at the top was highly significant.

- 6 times a winner at Mount Panorama, Bathurst, The Great Race
- 5 times a winner of the Australian Touring Car and Supercars Championships
- 90, yes, 90 race wins in the major league
- 41 Pole positions
- 88 times Mark graced the Podium
- 3 Australian Drivers Championships
- A member of the Supercars Hall Of Fame

The results are impressive and so was the effort and protocol to get there. Mark's engineering skills and technical understanding remain benchmark.

To this day his engineers are not only friends; they revere him and his ability to lift the bar. Engineering wizards like Ross Holder, Richard Hollway, David Swenson and Alastair McVean will readily recount the tremendous joint success and the number of debriefs that commenced with, 'You blokes must be kidding yourselves ...'

In my universe, the strongest memories are the weird little things, the odd moments shared rather than the turn-by turn-racing stories. Like the time I turned my Formula Holden into a bathtub off the end of the back straight at Sandown battling with him for pole. Winning that meant enough to risk having a 275 km/h shunt that could have killed me. Out of the rubble, he stopped to collect me and my steering wheel. Shaking, I rode back to the pit garage on the side pod of his race car.

LIFE AFTER RACING

We thankfully sustained no damage or injury speeding side by side through the dogleg at Oran Park in our Formula Holdens. We got away with it and giggled like idiots about it later.

Once at Eastern Creek, now Sydney Motorsport Park, somebody deposited oil everywhere. I arrived first on the scene in front of MS, slipping all over the joint like a dog on Lino. Glimpsing hurriedly in the mirror while trying not to have a giant crash here's boofhead signalling me with his animated hands to get on with it so we could resume our battle. *Urrghhh*.

After having the living daylights frightened out of me driving the Gibson Motorsport Nissan GT-R Godzilla in early Bathurst practice in 1992, Skaifey – urged on by Jim Richards – suggests the best medicine was a beer and maybe another? He was right.

We co-hosted a national radio show on Triple M called *The Stick Shift*. It was informative, crazy and great fun. The audience was massive, and the harder we tried to verbally 'fence' each other, the better it was. At least we thought so.

Shining the light on his racing success is a straightforward mission. What is less evident is Mark's mid-week backstory. Mark has served as a dedicated Supercars Board Member, Chaired the Supercars Commission, consulted to the governing body, Motorsport Australia (formerly CAMS), and worked with expert engineering consultants iEDM on track design and safety.

On a daily basis and for more than 35 years Mark has worked diligently to further the motor racing cause like few others have. His work ethic and attention to detail are punishing – especially for those that can't keep up.

Our time together began at Winton Motor Raceway, in North Eastern Victoria in 1985. Back then, we were both driving turbo-charged Mitsubishi Cordia Production cars. What started as our first proper lesson in front wheel drive torque steer laid the foundations for a long-standing friendship and partnership.

Thirty-five years later the serious business and sport of motor racing still compels us. The passion is palpable and the rapport remains evident and strong. His journey, our journey, involves more success than failure with a garnish of hard knocks, politics, great people and a few annoying pricks along the way.

These days, instead of engineering debriefs in a sweaty race suit, life is full of production meetings, host desks and research notes. Although his helmet has given way to studio lights, his original racing love remains 100% pure – still talking up the sport, the best drivers, the best teams, celebrating the skillset of today's heroes as they wring the best performance out of their cars while dancing between the guard rail.

As old mates, we still get to share the same giddy excitement and forensic analysis of the game just as we did in the mid '80s at the start. I enjoy and have always enjoyed the pleasure of his company and admire Mark Skaife as a celebrated and legendary competitor in the storied history of Australian motorsport. ◉

In our element: presenting to camera in the studio with Neil Crompton.

Jess Yates, yours truly, Craig Lowndes and Neil Crompton cover all the Supercars race action for FOX Sports viewers. Here, we're in pit lane on-air at the 2019 Clipsal 500 in Adelaide.

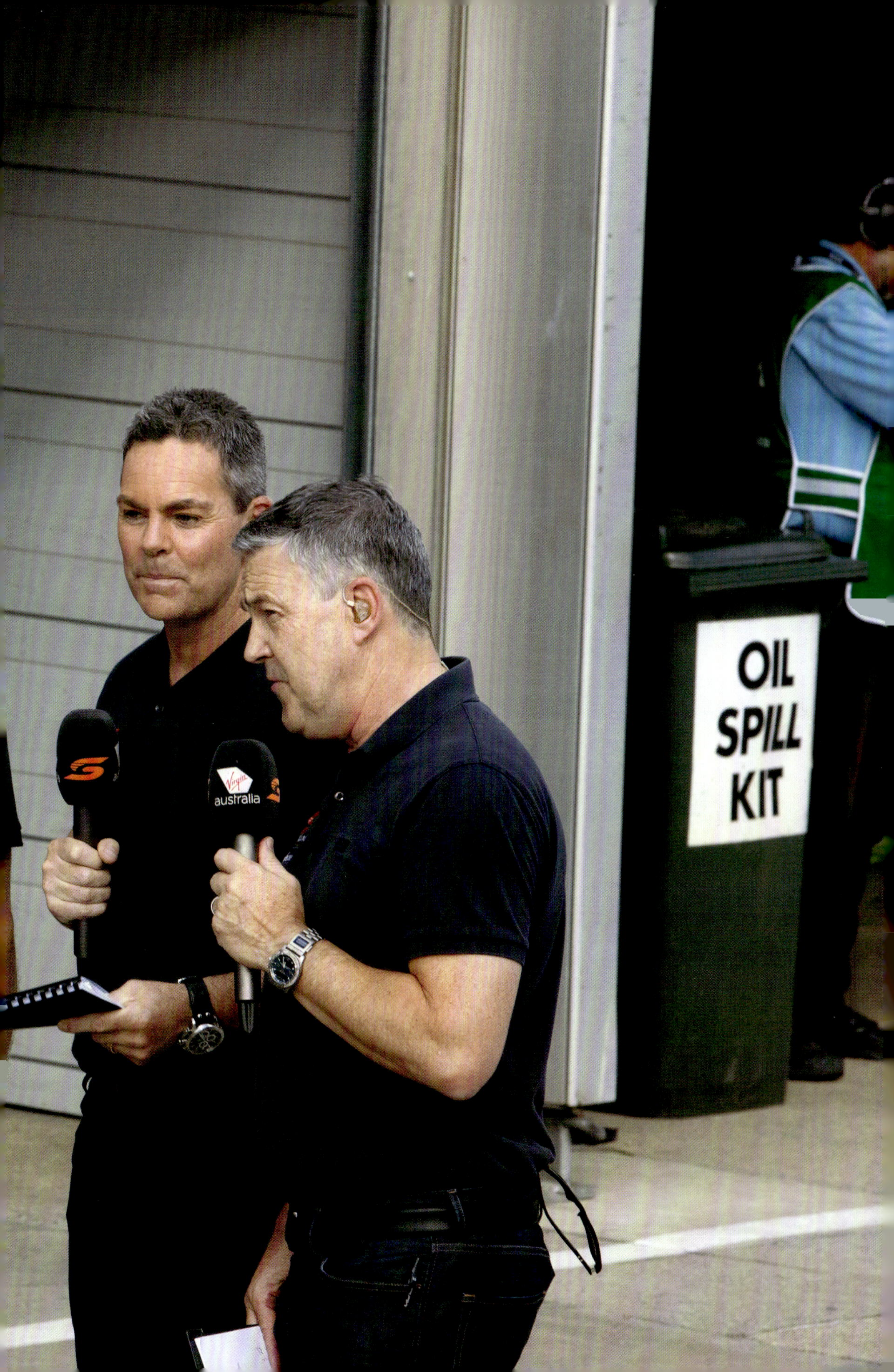
australia
OIL
SPILL
KIT

THE DEVIL IS IN THE DETAIL
Words by Jessica Yates, Fox Sports Australia Presenter

I grew up watching Mark's sporting prowess on TV. Bathurst and Skaifey were one and the same when I was a kid. He was that hardcore racer, win-at-all-costs-or-die-trying personality – and that's why Australians love him.

Long before I began working with Mark, I greatly admired his eloquent and polished broadcasting style and the ease with which he transitioned from athlete to expert, making the often technical and complex nature of car racing easy to understand. Ask anyone in the game: that attribute alone is worth its weight in gold. He's a champion, the very best we've witnessed who's won it all, with an intuitive sense of show biz, always striking the balance between entertaining and informing. That is a rare gem in television, and that's exactly what Mark is.

There is nothing accidental about Skaifey; the devil is in the detail. His ability to recount every fact, important number, every twist and turn of every race track in the country, every minute detail of Australian car racing, is his superpower. A superpower he has perfected through pure passion. It is his labour of love.

He treats our broadcast team like his race team, full of faith and high expectations of us to deliver. His competitive flair hasn't waned and it keeps us all on our toes. He likes to remind me when he's rightly predicted a race winner or pole sitter and I'm always happy to congratulate him on doing his job.

We have laughed from the very first day we had the good fortune to know each other. He tackles the broadcast itself like he would any Bathurst 1000. 'Live for the now, Jessica,' he says when debating which story we should chase and what our next move might be. That has become our mantra. It gives us great insight into why Mark has enjoyed so much success both on and off the track. He lives in the moment wholeheartedly, and that's been the best tonic for us all.

THE GIFTED RACE CALLER
Words by Steve Crawley, Head of Television, Fox Sports

As a champion driver, Mark's work ethic was legendary. But in my role as head of television at Fox Sports Australia, I best know him as a host and commentator. Of all the sportscasters I've worked with over 30 years none have worked harder, longer or smarter than Mark Skaife.

We believe he ranks among the best callers in world sport. He is almost definitely the best prepared. When you walk into the commentary box at Bathurst there are more numbers and names on more sheets of paper and laptops than in a cockpit at Cape Canaveral. True, we've never been in a cockpit at Cape Canaveral but we're painting a picture here.

He can tell you what happened on every bend in every race of any significance dating back to the early eighties, to when he was racing go karts. And he tells you with great excitement, insight and accuracy. 'You always remember the things you love,' says Mark from Wyong.

GET OUT OF THE CHAIR AND ONTO THE TRACK
Words by Craig Lowndes, racing driver and former teammate

Mark has been fantastic with my transition to commentary. Again, he is very detail-focused about what's going on, who's doing what, who's throwing to who and so on. So that side of it is very much the same philosophy as he applied to his driving.

When I first came on board he was extremely helpful, trying to get me up to speed as quickly as possible. We had a lot of phone calls prior to the Adelaide race, explaining what I'd encounter, what I needed to bring, what I should be looking for. The one big bit of advice he did give me was to get out of the chair between our on-camera stuff and get down to pit lane, literally do your reporting and don't get spoon-fed.

He loves a laugh, and he'll stitch you up if he gets the chance. From time to time the producer will be in my ear saying something like 'Mark will be talking at this point', and then he'll tell me, 'All right, no more time for you, CL. Mark will throw it to Jess, Jess will throw it down to whoever it was going to be next.' So I can be sitting there listening to Mark explain his opinion, he would then turn to me and say, 'So, what do you think CL?' He'd literally stitch me up knowing that there was no extra time to have a comment. And my reply would be either a yes or a no, and I'd basically have to let Jess just pick it up.

I think, like Jamie Whincup and Marcos Ambrose, he was misunderstood as a driver. His competitiveness and the need to get things right was often interpreted as arrogance. But he was so focused at the track he didn't have time for things like autographs and the like. He did relax more when he was part time with us in the end, and I think he enjoyed the sport for what it was.

The things that haven't changed are that he is always dressed immaculately, which we joke about all the time. And he likes to be in control: the commentary team's accommodation is usually Mark's recommendation, and then every time we go out for dinner at race weekends he is always the first to order the wine, which is great because the wines he orders are fantastic, but I don't know if that is just because he doesn't have to pay the bill.

Above: Looking very casual at the Gold Coast street race, shaking hands with V8 Supercars Chairman Tony Cochrane on becoming the inaugural V8 Supercars Commission Chairman.

Right: Speaking with Neil Crompton at the Car of the Future launch in 2012

LIFE AFTER RACING   247

The Car of the Future launch was the end of three years of work and it was a monumental body of work for a sport chasing a new product platform. It opened the door for manufacturers other than Ford or Holden to participate. The wall you can see on the left was one of my methods for mapping the development of the program.

V8 SUPERCARS
CAR OF THE FUTURE

RCARS
2013
DRIVEN BY DUNLOP
Energizer
V8 SUPERCARS
CAR OF THE FUTURE

Above: It was great to welcome Nissan back to the level of touring car racing in Australia, more than two decades after the very category it was joining had been created to kill the Nissan GT-R. To my left are Tony Cochrane (Supercars Chairman); David Malone (Supercars CEO); John Crennan (Nissan Motorsport CEO), Todd and Rick Kelly, whose team was switching to Nissan; Ian Moreillon (Nissan Sales Director); and Dan Thompson (Nissan MD).

Above: Sitting with Garry Rogers at the announcement of Volvo entering Supercars Racing with his team. The Volvo was a great example of how the Car of the Future platform could be adapted to allow non-traditional cars into the series.

MY REAL FAMILY

As you've read, my wife Toni's love, support and encouragement have been unflappable throughout my driving career and beyond. Most of my working life has been spent in workshops around a bunch of blokes – nothing could be further from that than being a father to two girls: Mia and Tilly. My first child, Mitch, was easier for me to understand.

The nature or nurture debate is a very interesting one. Understanding the girls and getting the best from them has been a challenge. Every Monday after I come home from a race meeting we go out for dinner, and we often have some really good chats there. Recently, for example, we spoke about what it is to be a good parent.

To me, I think our job as parents really is putting together all the things that you have to do – teach them manners, show a sense of care, educate them, help them with family values and all those other more abstract lessons that, when added together, equals being prepared for life – and in the end that's our job. To prepare them for life. On the paper tablecloth of the restaurant, I started to write all the things down and the girls were contributing too. It was actually one of the best discussions that I've ever had with them. They are getting into their teens now, and I'm finding it's an age where they like that sort of stuff and they get it too.

They are little clones of Toni, and being able to understand Toni has helped me immeasurably. Parenting is like trying to get the best out of a team, but on steroids. In terms of learning, yes, it's great to have a bike helmet on and we would all subscribe to having a bike helmet on. But the trick to riding a bike is not falling off. So prevention and the ability to learn from your mistakes are far better than a cure.

As a dad the first part is: 'Oh, did you hurt yourself?' And then the second part is: 'When did you do that? How did it happen?' Then follow up with: 'What do you do next time?'

Then they've got to learn to cope with Mark Skaife as a father at their sporting events. I've got to say, it is not good. There's a bit of déjà vu of *my* dad's feedback on my footy performances going on – I think the girls like me being there, but they don't like my game reviews or my input from the sidelines.

I remember when Mitch was still at school, and I was standing with the principal from the Peninsula School where he went. He was probably 16, and they were playing a really good football team like Marcellin College.

There were a couple of wild blokes on both sides and it started to get volatile. I was standing with the principal and we were having a bit of a laugh when one of Mitch's mates – Jack Connolly – was coming to the bench. One of the guys from the other side's bench sprayed water on him, and I yelled out, 'Belt him, Jack!' So, Jack turned around and belted him. It ended up as massive all-in brawl and the principal turned to me after it settled down and said, 'You started that.' That was a good example of Mark the bad father.

I've loved going to watch my kids play sport over the years – though they're not always so pleased to be getting my feedback from the sidelines …

ONE LUCKY GIRL
Words by Toni Skaife, General Manager Channel 10, and wife

I first met Mark Skaife in 1997 at Symmons Plains. I was 24, and never for a second did I think that he would become my husband seven years later, then the father of my children, or indeed the indelible life partner that he has become.

I was working at Network 10 on the V8 coverage, and he joined us for a spot in the commentary box during Gibson Motorsport's brief racing hiatus due to the contentious banning of tobacco advertising in Australian sport. Of course back then Gibsons was famously sponsored by the iconic Australian cigarette brand, and they were known legendarily as the 'Winfield Racing Team'. I know this, you see, because in 1991 and 1992, when Mark and Jimmy Richards won The Great Race at Bathurst in the Winfield Nissan, I was serendipitously there taking it all in. Not at Mount Panorama – 'the Mount', as it was known – but in the township of Bathurst itself.

I moved there at the beginning of 1991 when I was 17 years old to attend university. Not to detract from its rich historical significance, Bathurst was very much a university town, but each October it was taken over by racing enthusiasts – otherwise known to us students as 'hoons'. I looked at this annual spectacle of great Australian culture with a very different lens to the one I have today. Back then I cursed it. There was nowhere to park in town; the pubs and cafe (yes, there was only one – all the others were called coffee shops) were too full get a table. The town's population more than quadrupled, and the university students who had the usual run of the place would run and hide. I had not a speck of interest in motor racing.

Not even when, some years later, I begrudgingly took a role at Network 10 that required me to manage the production of the live V8 Supercar telecasts. I recall accepting that role for two reasons. One, I loved TV and desperately wanted to work at 10 – after all, it was home to all the shows I grew up with. Two, I thought that live event TV, albeit sport, would be a great grounding for my career (and I was right). However, there was a third reason (then unbeknownst to me), and that was to meet Mark. Yes, I am a believer in fate, and when I finally fell in love, I truly believed Mark Skaife was my destiny and that the universe had delivered him to me. I still do.

None of my friends believed me when I first told them we had started dating. I liked going to the theatre, to film festivals and on picnics, not to the race track! But

I soon learned to love it, now that it was so much more than work for me. It was exhilarating to watch Mark, this master on his own stage. Those days of watching him race and being in the inner sanctum of it all were a real honour. He truly was masterful.

I'm so proud of Mark. Not only for his on-track talents, but for his off-track record too. He has produced three outstanding young people in his children. Each one of them resembles him in some special way, but all of them his share his deep sense of loyalty, his drive and his slapstick sense of humour. Mitch, my stepson, is just gold. I've been telling him since he was five years old, 'Don't go changin', Mitch,' – you know, like the Billy Joel song? He always laughs like it's a daggy joke we share, but I kind of mean it. When I married Mark, Mitch was 11; he wore the same suit and tie as his dad, and he stood by Mark's side facing me, as I made my vows to them both. Mitch is all heart.

And then there are Mimi (Mia) and Tilly, 14 and 12. Both of them are pure joy and have completed our family. They came along toward the end of Mark's career and so they don't have a lot of racing memories, but they enjoy the stories and watching the replays on Fox Sports. To them, Mark is Daddy, and he is an awesome one at that. Like my dad was for me, he's an advocate for girls to do anything and to follow their dreams no matter how lofty or how ordinary. He instills in them the need to be fair, honest and to work hard for what you want and what is right.

It's no surprise these three children love their dad so much; he is present in their lives and gives himself to them.

For 20 years, we have been by each other's sides, and boy, it has been a hell of a ride. Since 2000, when our relationship began, there has been a gratifying intensity in my life. Mark's loyalty, his passion, his generosity, his optimism and his annoying pursuit of perfection are all defining traits of his, but the most remarkable trait of all is his commitment. His commitment to life, to the love of his sport, to always doing the right thing, and his commitment to us lucky ones he holds dear. He is an extraordinary human, and I'm one lucky girl.◉

Top left: Eastern Creek 2007 – celebrating breaking the record for round wins with Toni. She was pregnant with Tilly at the time and still managing the stress of my car racing. A deadset hero!

Top right: Toni with Mia and Tilly outside our hotel in Paris in 2018.

Bottom right: Toni with Mitch and our friend Chantal De Fraga at my 50th birthday bash.

LIFE AFTER RACING 255

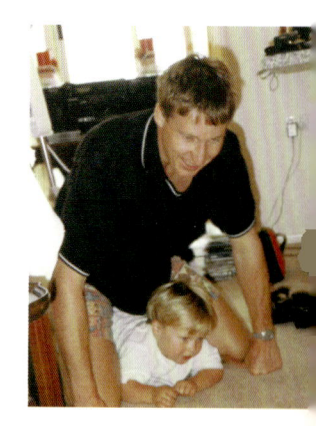

Mitch was born in June 1995. These photos are a glimpse into my journey with him, including a very special moment with the Olympic Torch I ran with in 2000. As he grew up, it was great to see him hanging out with Mum and Dad and his younger sisters.

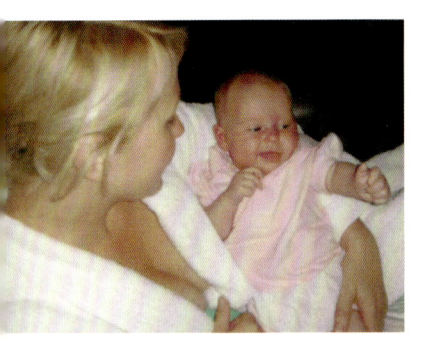

aving spent my career surrounded by blokes, I faced a whole new learning curve as the father two girls. From top left you can see Mia as a baby in 2006 and then taking her first early eps at the beach. There's Tilly in a helicopter going to Falls Creek with one my best mates ark Tucker and me (*top right*), Tilly and Mia on the flying Kangaroo coming back from South rica (*middle right, 2016*), Mia and Tilly with Mitch at Mia's 12th birthday dinner at Nobu ottom right, 2018), and Toni and me skiing at Hotham with the girls and Mark Tucker ottom left). Finally there's me with my fellow dads and great friends (from left) Andrew unlop, Jon De Fraga and Pete Murray, helping out with Mother's Day activities at the kids' school.

LIFE AFTER RACING   257

CIRCUIT DESIGN

The circuit design and engineering is the work we underestimated in *'Skaife Next'*, and I've enjoyed it. We have done some permanent facilities, but most have been temporary or street circuits. We've also helped with modifications to existing tracks, like moving the pits at Barbagallo or modernising Pukekohe by adding the chicane on the back straight to add another passing point, as well as using some of the safety infrastructure from Hamilton.

The first street circuit I did was in Canberra and I've been working on them ever since, including in other cities like Newcastle. Sydney Olympic Park was a ripper. On paper it looked like an average race track but it was really cool because we did a lot of design stuff to increase the challenge. Townsville was also a good project because we got to add some purpose-built stuff to go with the street component.

I've also been working on a couple of tracks that will still be in development when this book is released. One is probably the biggest automotive development in Australia in a very long time and it is being built at Brisbane Airport. It isn't a race track as such, but it will comprise a complete test track with skid pans and the like inside a massive automotive precinct. It will only be a test track and will be accredited by FIA at that level, but that has been a great project that will promote economic growth for decades.

There are other projects in Queensland and Victoria that might have funding by publication too … A lot of my design work is sort of similar to what Greg Norman does in golf course design, effectively. What I am trying to do is create tracks that feature the best scenarios around interesting corners – tracks that possess a sense of character and penalise mistakes, all with certain safety levels embedded.

And it all gets you thinking. I look at what they've done in Newcastle and I wonder what we could do in Geelong, for instance. How many other sports can bring that many people and that much attention to a place like that? But the Newcastle people were great; we were able to do so many things to make that track, like build retaining walls beside the beach so we could construct a road on top of it. They are seriously committed to racing there and it shows. They are a great example of how to do it.

We do a really good job of motor racing for a region with such a small population. Outside Europe I would argue we are the most sophisticated motorsport precinct in the world.

In Townsville we were able to blend a street circuit with a section of purpose-built race track to be the only hybrid design in Australia, and the end result was amazing. Based on the action we have seen at this corner over the years, the corporate stand at the end of the main straight at Townsville (*above*), is one of the best positions to watch the racing.

The track at Sydney Olympic Park posed many challenges in terms of what we were allowed to do and where we were allowed to put the track, but with the team at iEDM we made a track that produced some great racing. This is the braking zone for the first corner at the end of Australia Avenue.

LIFE AFTER RACING 261

The Newcastle track is a great example of a council or government committing to a motor racing project 100 per cent, and the result is one of the most spectacular tracks on our tour. The run down Shortland Esplanade to the Newcastle Surf Club is one of the most picturesque and challenging strips of road anywhere we go.

LIFE AFTER RACING 263

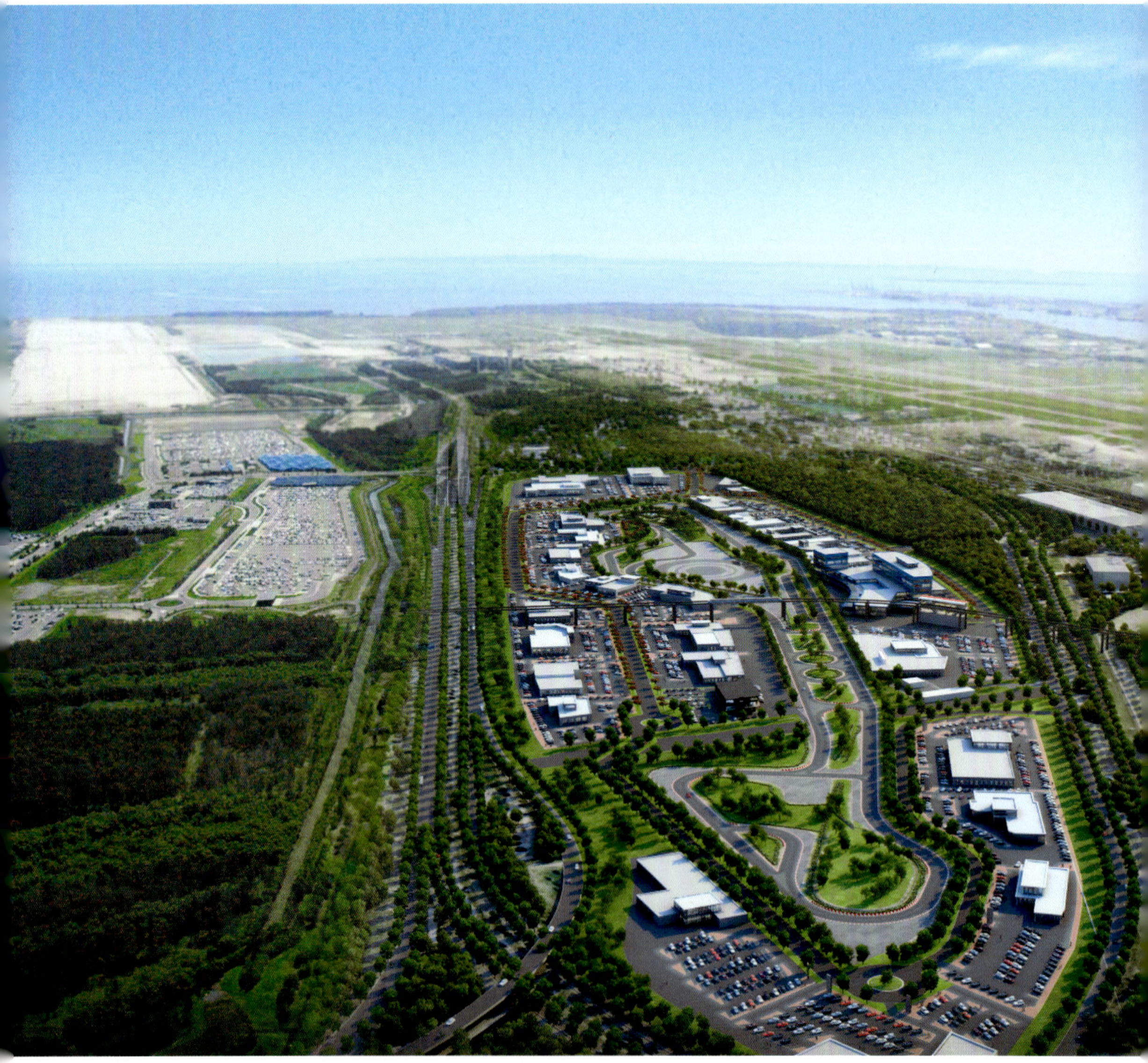

The Brisbane Auto Mall is a very exciting project in which I have been involved. As these artists' impressions show, it is a 55-hectare site within the Brisbane Airport precinct that will be the new epicentre for automotive retailing and test-drive experience, with a 2.5km circuit designed in the middle of the complex. This facility will be the benchmark in Australia and is scheduled to open in late-2022.

SKAIFE: AN EPIC DYNASTY OF AUSTRALIAN MOTORSPORT
Words by Andrew Clarke, motorsport journalist

Mark Skaife is quite a unique person. He is one of the hardest and most driven competitors I have seen in my more than 30 years covering motorsport, but he is also someone who cares deeply for the various layers that matter to him: family, team and his broader set of colleagues have driven decisions by the heart, with control eventually from the head.

My journey in motorsport started at around the same time as Mark's, so I have watched him grow from that young and brash 20-something through his years as a champion into a leader of his sport off the track. He has learned many lessons along the way, but through it he changed the face of motorsport with his intense level of competition and analytical mind. For many years, if you wanted to win you first needed to beat Mark Skaife.

He was simultaneously both the enemy and the chosen one – depending on which brand you followed – and some even in the same camp didn't warm to him … but that was the cost of doing business and being the best. The stats sheet puts him among the greatest drivers to have raced touring cars in Australia. Perhaps an army of racers stood on the side of the track – or perhaps, more importantly in this millennium, watched from inside his car via race cam – and admired his craft the way Mark admired his first batch of idols in the late 1970s and early 1980s.

Today his life is perhaps even more chaotic than it was when he was racing. His work with Foxtel covering the sport takes time and effort, but then there is a pile of other work and plenty of people seeking his advice that keeps him going for hours a day. But he needs a desk, a place to switch on and commit like he did with the headlights in his racing days. Headlights on for a qualifying lap.

It is not my job here to grade greatness. Suffice to say that anyone who doesn't have Skaife either at the top or near its peak when ranking the best we have seen, clearly doesn't understand the sport.

I have many stories of that intense warrior. Some good, some not so good … some even funny. I still remember hunting him down after the incident in Perth you will read about, I joined him for the walk back to his tent and he looked at me with that trademark intensity, and a little humour, and simply asked, 'Are you here to wind me up?' Not as such, but it did always help the quotes if you could get him on the rev limiter.

Our relationship is one, I hope, of mutual respect. There are few I admire in any sport as much as Mark, for the way he applied himself week-in, week-out for decades and extracted the very best from himself and those around him.

He was as brutal on the track as he was quick witted with his acid tongue, and therein lay the reason he polarised some onlookers. Whether you like him as a person doesn't really matter that much, but you have to be impressed by what he achieved and his dedication to achieving what he did. The reaction even from Ford fans in his final handful of rounds revealed that while many disliked him, they couldn't help but admire him.

I hope this is not the last book he writes because there is so much more to tell – and time passing will allow those stories to come to light.

My final race at Bathurst was in this stunning BMW M6 in the 2017 Bathurst 12 Hour race, sharing the driving with Tony Longhurst, Russell Ingall and Timo Glock. We qualified eighth on the grid but pulled out after 134 laps.

MARK SKAIFE CHRONOLOGY AND KEY CAREER STATISTICS

CHRONOLOGY

1967
- Born 3 April in Gosford, New South Wales

1981
- Started racing go-karts

1984
- First car race at Amaroo Park – Holden Torana XU-1 Sports Sedan

1985
- New South Wales Laser Series – #2nd for Tyretown Racing

1986
- New South Wales Laser Series – #2nd for Tyretown Racing
- Victorian Laser Series – 1st for Tyretown Racing
- Bathurst – Mark Skaife/Peter Williamson – DNS – Toyota Supra

1987
- Australian Touring Car Championship (ATCC) – 17th (12 points) – 0 Wins / 0 Podiums / 0 Poles – 1 of 9 Rounds – Nissan Gazelle for Peter Jackson Nissan Racing (Gibson Motor Sport)
- Australian 2.0 Litre Touring Car Championship – 1st – Nissan Gazelle for Peter Jackson Nissan Racing (Gibson Motor Sport)
- Bathurst – Mark Skaife/Grant Jarrett – 19th – Nissan Gazelle for Peter Jackson Nissan Racing (Gibson Motor Sport)

1988
- ATCC – Equal 28th (0 points) – 0 Wins / 0 Podiums / 0 Poles – 1 of 8 Rounds – Nissan Skyline HR31 GTS-R for Peter Jackson Nissan Racing (Gibson Motor Sport)
- Bathurst – Mark Skaife/George Fury – DNF – Nissan Skyline HR31 GTS-R for Peter Jackson Nissan Racing (Gibson Motor Sport)

1989
- ATCC – 9th (22 points) – 0 Wins / 1 Podiums / 0 Poles – 8 of 8 Rounds – Nissan Skyline HR31 GTS-R for Nissan Motorsport Australia (Gibson Motor Sport)
- Bathurst – Mark Skaife/Jim Richards – 3rd – Nissan Skyline HR31 GTS-R for Nissan Motorsport Australia (Gibson Motor Sport)

1990
- ATCC – 14th (9 points) – 0 Wins / 0 Podiums / 0 Poles – 8 of 8 Rounds, Rounds 1-5, 8 – Nissan Skyline HR31 GTSR, Rounds 6-7 in Nissan Skyline BNR32 GT-R for Nissan Motorsport Australia (Gibson Motor Sport)

- Bathurst – Mark Skaife/Jim Richards – 18th – Nissan GT-R for Nissan Motorsport Australia (Gibson Motor Sport)
- Australian Drivers' Championship (ADC) – 3rd (23 Points) – 0 Wins / 2 Podiums – 5 of 8 Rounds – Spa FB001 for Skaife Racing (Gibson Motor Sport)

1991
- ATCC – 2nd (132 points) – 3 Wins / 8 Podiums / 3 Poles – 9 of 9 Rounds – Nissan Skyline BNR32 GT-R for Nissan Motorsport Australia (Gibson Motor Sport)
- Bathurst – Mark Skaife/Jim Richards – 1st – Nissan BNR32 GT-R for Nissan Motorsport Australia (Gibson Motor Sport)
- ADC – 1st (135 Points) – 6 Wins/ 7 Podiums – 7 of 7 Rounds in Spa FB003 for Skaife Racing (Gibson Motor Sport)

1992
- ATCC – 1st (234 points) – 4 Wins / 7 Podiums / 2 Poles – 9 of 9 Rounds – Nissan Skyline BNR32 GT-R for Winfield Team Nissan (Gibson Motor Sport)
- Bathurst – Mark Skaife/Jim Richards – 1st – Nissan Skyline BNR32 GT-R for Winfield Team Nissan (Gibson Motor Sport)
- ADC – 1st (90 Points) – 3 Wins / 5 Podiums – 5 of 5 Rounds – SPA FB003 for Winfield Racing (Gibson Motor Sport)
- FIA Formula 3000 International Championship – 29th – Reynard 92D Mugen Honda for 3001 International

1993
- ATCC – 6th (87 points) – 0 Wins / 2 Podiums / 2 Poles – 9 of 9 Rounds – Holden VP Commodore for Winfield Racing (Gibson Motor Sport)
- Bathurst – Mark Skaife/Jim Richards – 2nd – Holden VP Commodore for Winfield Racing (Gibson Motor Sport)
- ADC – 1st (110 Points) – 4 Wins / 5 Podiums – 6 of 6 Rounds – Lola T91/50 Holden for Winfield Racing (Gibson Motor Sport)
- Married Belinda, 13 November

1994
- ATCC – 1st (285 points) – 4 Wins / 8 Podiums / 3 Poles – 10 of 10 Rounds – Holden VP Commodore for Gibson Motor Sport
- Bathurst – Mark Skaife/Jim Richards – DNF – Holden VP Commodore for Gibson Motor Sport

1995
- ATCC – 6th (145 points) – 1 Wins / 2 Podiums / 0 Poles – 9 of 10 Rounds – Holden VR Commodore for Gibson Motor Sport
- Bathurst – Mark Skaife/Jim Richards – DNF – Holden VR Commodore for Gibson Motor Sport

- ADC – 7th (32 Points) – 0 Wins / 2 Podiums – 2 of 6 Rounds – Lola T93/50 for Gibson Motor Sport
- Mitch born, 13 June

1996
- ATCC – 9th (177 points) – 0 Wins / 1 Podiums / 0 Poles – 10 of 10 Rounds – Holden VR Commodore for Gibson Motor Sport
- Bathurst – Mark Skaife/John Cleland – 7th – Holden VR Commodore for Gibson Team Sega

1997
- ATCC – 13th (166 points) – 0 Wins / 1 Podiums / 0 Poles – 5 of 10 Rounds – Holden VS Commodore for Gibson Motor Sport
- Bathurst – Mark Skaife/Peter Brock – DNF – Holden VS Commodore for Holden Racing Team 1998 – (Not including Sandown 500 & Bathurst 1000)

1998
- ATCC – 3rd (768 points) – 0 Wins / 4 Podiums / 5 Poles – 10 of 10 Rounds – Holden VS Commodore for Holden Racing Team
- Bathurst – Mark Skaife/Craig Lowndes – 5th – Holden Racing Team

1999
- V8 Supercar Championship Series/ATCC (V8SCS) – 3rd (1656 points) – 6 Wins / 7 Podiums / 2 Poles – 13 of 13 Rounds – Holden VT Commodore for Holden Racing Team
- Bathurst – Mark Skaife/Paul Morris – 3rd – Holden VT Commodore for Holden Racing Team

2000
- V8SCS – 1st (1570 points) – 4 Wins / 8 Podiums / 3 Poles – 13 of 13 Rounds – Holden VT Commodore for Holden Racing Team
- Bathurst – Mark Skaife/Craig Lowndes – 6th – Holden VT Commodore for Holden Racing Team

2001
- V8SCS – 1st (3478 points) – 4 Wins / 9 Podiums / 4 Poles – 13 of 13 Rounds – Holden VX Commodore for Holden Racing Team
- Bathurst – Mark Skaife/Tony Longhurst – 1st – Holden VX Commodore for Holden Racing Team

2002
- V8SCS – Mark Skaife – 1st (2227 points) – 7 Wins / 8 Podiums / 5 Poles – 13 of 13 Rounds – Holden VX Commodore for Holden Racing Team
- Bathurst – Mark Skaife/Jim Richards – 1st – Holden VX Commodore for Holden Racing Team

2003
- V8SCS – 3rd (1853 points) – 2 Wins / 6 Podiums / 3 Poles – 13 of 13 Rounds – Holden VY Commodore for Holden Racing Team
- Bathurst – Mark Skaife/Todd Kelly – 8th – Holden VY Commodore for Holden Racing Team

2004
- V8SCS – 12th (1294 points) – 0 Wins / 1 Podiums / 3 Poles – 13 of 13 Rounds – Holden VY Commodore for Holden Racing Team
- Bathurst – Mark Skaife/Todd Kelly – 14th – Holden VY Commodore for Holden Racing Team
- Married Toni, 21 August

2005
- V8SCS – 5th (1754 points) – 1 Wins / 4 Podiums / 2 Poles – 13 of 13 Rounds – Holden VZ Commodore for Holden Racing Team
- Bathurst – Mark Skaife/Todd Kelly – 1st – Holden VZ Commodore for Holden Racing Team

2006
- V8SCS – 16th (2036 points) – 1 Wins / 3 Podiums / 4 Poles – 13 of 13 Rounds – Holden VZ Commodore for Holden Racing Team
- Bathurst – Mark Skaife/Garth Tander – DNF – Holden VZ Commodore for Holden Racing Team
- Mia born, 10 March

2007
- V8SCS – 8th (379 points) – 1 Wins / 3 Podiums / 0 Poles – 13 of 14 Rounds Holden VE Commodore for Holden Racing Team
- Bathurst – Mark Skaife/Todd Kelly – DNF – Holden VE Commodore for Holden Racing Team

2008
- V8SCS – 14th (1644 points) – 1 Wins / 1 Podiums / 0 Poles – 14 of 14 Rounds – Holden VE Commodore for Holden Racing Team
- Bathurst – Mark Skaife/Garth Tander – 12th – Holden VE Commodore for Holden Racing Team
- Tilly born, 24 October

2009
- V8SCS – 31st (372 points) – 0 Wins / 0 Podiums / 0 Poles – 2 of 14 Rounds – Holden VE Commodore for Sprint Gas Racing (Tasman Motorsport)
- Bathurst – Mark Skaife/Greg Murphy – 4th – Holden VE Commodore for Sprint Gas Racing (Tasman Motorsport)

2010
- V8SCS – 33rd (560 points) – 2 Wins / 2 Podiums / 0 Poles – 2 of 14 Rounds – Holden VE Commodore for Team Vodafone (Triple Right Race Engineering)
- Bathurst – Mark Skaife/Craig Lowndes – 1st – Holden VE Commodore for Team Vodafone (Triple Eight Race Engineering)

2011
- V8SCS – 29th (532 points) – 1 Wins / 2 Podiums / 0 Poles – 2 of 14 Rounds – Holden VE Commodore for Team Vodafone (Triple Right Race Engineering)
- Bathurst – Mark Skaife/Craig Lowndes – 2nd – Holden VE Commodore for Team Vodafone (Triple Eight Race Engineering)

2012
- Australian Carrera Cup Championship - 21st (58 Points) – 1 round of 8 - Porsche 997 GT3 Cup for Porsche Cars Australia

2017
- Bathurst 12 Hour – Mark Skaife/Timo Glock/Russell Ingall/Tony Longhurst - DNF – BMW M6 GT3 for BMW Team SRM

KEY CAREER STATISTICS

- ATCC / V8SCS – 220 Rounds/482 Races – 5 Championships (92, 94, 00, 01, 02) – 42 Round Wins / 90 Race Wins / 88 Podiums / 41 Poles
- Bathurst – 25* Starts – 6 Wins (91, 92, 01, 02, 05 & 10) / 10 Podiums / 5 Poles
  * Mark did not start the race in 1986 despite qualifying
- ADC – 25 Starts – 3 Championships (91, 92, 93) – 15 Wins / 21 Podiums

AUSTRALIAN TOURING CAR/V8 SUPERCAR CHAMPIONSHIP OVERVIEW

Milestones

1st Round	1987 Sandown
50th Round	1995 Symmons Plains
100th Round	2000 Eastern Creek
150th Round	2004 Eastern Creek
200th Round	2007 Phillip Island
Last Round	2011 Bathurst

Teams

Gibson Motorsport	73 rounds	1987–1997
Holden Racing Team	141 rounds	1998–2008
Tasman Motorsport	2 rounds	2009
Triple Eight Race Engineering	4 rounds	2010–2011

At a glance

Round Starts	220
Round Wins	42
Race Starts	479
Race Wins	90
First Race Win	1991 Wanneroo
Last Race Win	2011 Phillip Island
Finishing Rate	88.3% (423 finishes from 479 races)
Podium Finishes	88
First Podium	1989 Winton
Last Podium	2011 Bathurst
Pole Positions	41
First Pole Position	1991 Mallala
Last Pole Position	2006 Symmons Plains
Championship Wins	5 (1992, 1994, 2000, 2001, 2002)

RACE WINS BY TRACK

Track	Race wins	First win	Last win
Adelaide	4	2000	2003
Amaroo Park	3	1992	1994
Barbagallo/Wanneroo	8	1991	2006
Bathurst	5	1995	2010
Calder Park	1	1999	1999
Canberra	3	2001	2002
Eastern Creek	10	1995	2007
Hidden Valley	8	2000	2007
Mallala	5	1991	1994
Oran Park	15	1991	2007
Phillip Island	9	1998	2011

Track	Race wins	First win	Last win
Pukukohe	4	2002	2006
Queensland Railway	2	2000	2006
Sandown	6	1994	2003
Shanghai	1	2005	2005
Symmons Plains	4	1994	1999
Winton	2	1992	1992

Notes

- Skaife only competed in one round in 1987 and one round in 1988.
- Skaife competed in four rounds of the eight in the 1989 championship.
- Skaife's car was withdrawn from the 1990 round at Phillip Island after an accident in practice prior to the round's official commencement.
- Skaife drove a Skyline GTS-R in 1990 in all of his starts bar one - at Mallala he drove the GT-R.
- Skaife missed the opening round in 1995 at Sandown due to injuries sustained in an accident at the Triple Challenge at Eastern Creek.
- Skaife competed in five rounds of the 10 held in 1997 due to a lack of sponsorship.
- Skaife missed the 2007 Sandown 500 due to an appendix operation during race week.
- Championship podiums were determined by round results up to the end of 2008 and by race results from 2009 onwards.

COMPLETE BATHURST 1000 RESULTS

Year	#	Team	Drivers	Car	Result
1986	77	Peter Williamson Toyota	Peter Williamson	Toyota Supra	DNS
1987	60	Peter Jackson Nissan Racing	Grant Jarrett	Nissan Gazelle	19th
1988	30	Peter Jackson Nissan Racing	George Fury	Nissan Skyline GTS-R	DNF
1989	2	Nissan Motorsport Australia	Jim Richards	Nissan Skyline GTS-R	3rd

Year	#	Team	Drivers	Car	Result
1990	1	Nissan Motorsport Australia	Jim Richards	Nissan Skyline GT-R	18th
1991	1	Nissan Motorsport Australia	Jim Richards	Nissan Skyline GT-R	1st
	2	Nissan Motorsport Australia	Drew Price/ Garry Waldon	Nissan Skyline GT-R	DNF
1992	1	Winfield Team Nissan	Jim Richards	Nissan Skyline GT-R	1st
1993	1	Winfield Racing Team	Jim Richards	Holden VP Commodore	2nd
1994	2	Winfield Racing	Jim Richards	Holden VP Commodore	DNF
1995	1	Winfield Racing	Jim Richards	Holden VR Commodore	DNF
1996	2	Gibson Motorsport	John Cleland	Holden VR Commodore	7th
1997	05	Holden Racing Team	Peter Brock	Holden VS Commodore	DNF
1998	1	Holden Racing Team	Craig Lowndes	Holden VT Commodore	6th
1999	2	Holden Racing Team	Paul Morris	Holden VT Commodore	3rd
2000	1	Holden Racing Team	Craig Lowndes	Holden VT Commodore	6th
2001	1	Holden Racing Team	Tony Longhurst	Holden VX Commodore	1st
2002	1	Holden Racing Team	Jim Richards	Holden VX Commodore	1st
2003	1	Holden Racing Team	Todd Kelly	Holden VY Commodore	8th
2004	2	Holden Racing Team	Todd Kelly	Holden VY Commodore	14th
2005	2	Holden Racing Team	Todd Kelly	Holden VZ Commodore	1st
2006	2	Holden Racing Team	Garth Tander	Holden VZ Commodore	DNF

Year	#	Team	Drivers	Car	Result
2007	2	Holden Racing Team	Todd Kelly	Holden VE Commodore	DNF
2008	1	Holden Racing Team	Garth Tander	Holden VE Commodore	12th
2009	51	Tasman Motorsport	Greg Murphy	Holden VE Commodore	4th
2010	888	Triple Eight Race Engineering	Craig Lowndes	Holden VE Commodore	1st
2011	888	Triple Eight Race Engineering	Craig Lowndes	Holden VE Commodore	2nd

ACKNOWLEDGEMENTS

As you would expect, pulling a book like this together has taken a massive team effort, so I would like to thank a few people who have helped with the end product.

Starting with Andrew Clarke, for all his tireless work in helping me get the detail and the storytelling correct. He certainly knows how painful I can be with ensuring a piece of work is as good as possible; many thanks, mate.

To Aaron Noonan for his help with some of the images and pulling together the career statistics; sincere thank you, Noons.

To Ruby, Freya, Martin and the team at Affirm Press, thank you for your patience and understanding in what has been a tumultuous year for everyone.

To Tony Box, head of talent at TLA (my management group) and one of the brains behind Ned's business, thanks for getting your team – specifically Samantha McLaughlin, Cassandra Burton and Laura McLachlan – to assist with the contributors and overall organisation; tremendous effort, Boxy.

Finally, to all my racing peers, work colleagues and family and friends who have contributed the anecdotes for this project, thank you very much for your contributions. Your kind words mean so much to me, and your stories – and the odd spray – will stay with me forever!

IMAGE CREDITS

The image on page 126 is courtesy of Marshall Cass/Autopics. The images on pages 26–27 are courtesy of Lance J Ruting/Autopics. The top-right image on page 111 is courtesy of Sutton Images/Motorsport Images. All images on pages 264–265 are courtesy of BNE.

Images on the following pages are courtesy of Aaron Noonan/an1images.com: 24, 33 (top), 37, 44, 46 (all), 49–51, 59–60, 64, 72, 75 (both), 80, 83, 85–86, 87 (bottom left), 88, 91 top, 93–94, 98, 101, 103–104, 106–107, 114, 116, 125, 128 (both), 130, 133, 144–145, 148, 154, 166, 168, 170, 172, 174–175, 179, 195–196, 198, 201–202, 204, 206, 208 (both), 211 (both), 214, 219, 222, 226, 228–230, 237, 242 and 268.

All other images supplied by Mark Skaife and TLA Management.